Archbishop's Diary

DAVID WILBOURNE is Domestic Chaplain to the Archbishop of York and Director of Ordinands in the York Diocese. Previously he was a parish priest near Pontefract and before that in Middlesbrough. Apart from six years studying in Cambridge he has lived in Yorkshire for most of his life.

JOHN HABGOOD became Archbishop of York in 1983, retiring in 1995. Prior to becoming Archbishop he was Bishop of Durham, Principal of Queen's Theological College, Birmingham, Vicar of Jedburgh (near Edinburgh), Vice Principal of Westcott House, Cambridge, and assistant curate in Kensington. Before his ordination in 1954 he was a research scientist at King's College, Cambridge, where he lectured in pharmacology and physiology.

Also published by SPCK,
two books by John Habgood:

Confessions of a Conservative Liberal (1988)

Making Sense (1993)

ARCHBISHOP'S DIARY

A year with John Habgood

DAVID WILBOURNE

First published 1995
SPCK
Holy Trinity Church
Marylebone Road
London
NW1 4DU

Copyright © David Wilbourne 1995

British Library Cataloguing in Publication Data
A catalogue record for this book is available from the British Library.

ISBN   0-281-04845-2

Typeset by Rowland Phototypesetting Limited,
Bury St Edmunds, Suffolk
Printed in Great Britain by
BPC Paperbacks Ltd

To mark the memory of my wife's cousin,

Richard William Glossop

1958–1992,

and his laughter.

CONTENTS

FOREWORD

by the Archbishop of York

David Wilbourne did not tell me what he was doing until his diary was well under way. As Dame Edna Everage might have said, there is something a bit spooky about having one's diary written by someone else. But I forgave him and I welcome its publication.

There are many aspects of an archbishop's life which receive little publicity—among them the continual programme of visits to parishes and cathedrals for which David usually accompanies me. This book celebrates that aspect of my ministry, and I hope gives something of its flavour, as a kind of pilgrimage around the North and a cherishing of its Church. David is a sharp observer with a wry sense of humour, so the portrait is not all flattering. But it is distinctly his and not mine.

To fit in with the general scheme of the book, some dates and places have had to be rearranged; but all events described have their origin in real life.

It is a good life, even though climbing into a car at the end of a day's work to go and preach one's umpteenth centenary sermon can at times induce a sense of depression. In fact such occasions almost always turn out to be enjoyable. And I am grateful to those whose careful preparation and warm response makes my own ministry possible. If I was allowed to dedicate David's book to someone of my choice, I would dedicate it to them, the clergy and people of the Province of York.

John Ebor:

PREFACE

John Habgood as Archbishop of York has a consistently high public profile. But I am also only too well aware of occasions which do not grab the headlines. These latter events are worthy of a wider audience and appreciation because they are not without substantial humour and pathos. This diary celebrates a selection of them as we go through a final year.

I have been chaplain for just over three years and I have drawn from my experience over that period for entries for this diary. To truncate three years into one year inevitably means that some dates and places have had to be rearranged. John's Gospel charts Jesus' ministry as spanning three years; in the other Gospels that same ministry spans just one year. Clearly truncating three into one is not without precedent!

ACKNOWLEDGEMENTS

To John Habgood for sharing himself, and for his generosity and trust in giving permission for this work to be written.

To my wife, Rachel, and Ruth, Hannah, and Clare, our daughters, for their love and liveliness.

To my Father for sharing his priesthood and my Mother for being herself.

To Margaret Cundiff who consistently encouraged the venture and Rachel Boulding, Senior Editor at SPCK, who likewise enthused.

To Mary, Anne, and Lynda at the Palace Secretariat who taught me the mysteries of the word processor and who with Raymond Barker encouraged the laughter.

To all those encountered in this diary.

SUMMER

15 JULY

'To begin is to end.' Beginning your final year as Archbishop by preaching at the memorial service of your predecessor has irresistible echoes of T. S. Eliot, John Habgood's favourite poet. The broad sweep John Habgood painted of Stuart Blanch's life was kindly, perceptive, and mostly accurate. Surprisingly though for a scientist, too much was often read into too little evidence: it did not necessarily follow that Lord Blanch of Bishopthorpe hated Bishopthorpe because he could not stand the purple carpet in the palace drawing-room!

Despite the warm summer's day, the service chilled the soul. The small congregation huddled in the choir of York Minster: surely more people should have turned out to mark this 'much loved archbishop'? The choir sang reasonably well, yet it was all routine stuff performed on automatic pilot. Donne's prayer was read with great effect, until the reader tripped over his words because of a mistype in the text: didn't the former archbishop warrant a rehearsal? And the sermon, though good, lacked tears, had nothing to make you pause and say, 'See how much he must have loved him.'

John Habgood: so much at the centre of things, indeed often the very definition of that centre, with the whiff of immortality about him. Yet was this how it would be in ten or so years' time at another death, an Archbishop largely forgotten by a church going through the motions? The ghost of the future haunted us all that day. And more than that, drove me to record a year.

16 JULY

The Archbishop at home, a Palace Open Day in aid of the new church hall. The continuing high summer brought out the crowds, locals thrilled to look behind the scenes of 'their palace', tourists bewildered by a rustic river trip whose stopover took them to the very heart of the Church of England.

The white-jacketed Archbishop humbly acted as guide, holding his group enthralled as he unfolded history with the skill of a born teacher. His spiel began with a slightly anxious moment as he assured his group how much the palace was used. An office, a home, private flats, a diocesan meeting room, official entertaining (after all the Prince and Princess of Wales had stayed here in 1866). The palace was clearly put to such a galaxy of uses that the Church Commissioners' angel of death could happily pass over its closure.

The group inevitably lapped it all up, starry-eyed. I remained unconvinced. The vast grounds uninhabited by humanity for nearly all the year deeply troubled me: gardens of Eden should throng with folk, especially when the heart of your gospel is the Fall redeemed.

19 JULY

The Senior Staff (who meet monthly to manage appointments and other diocesan affairs) featured in a strange nightmare which somehow merged with *The Jungle Book* and *The Wizard of Oz*. The Archbishop, perhaps inevitably, was a well-worn lion, the definite king of the diocesan jungle. The three suffragan bishops and archdeacons were less well-worn and appeared as six rather grumpy elephants. The other members of the Senior Staff were cast as five fleas. A furious discussion took place, with much trumpeting by the elephants, about whether the Senior Staff should co-opt an extra flea, so that each elephant could have one of its own. When the discussion moved on to whether the flea should be male or female, one elephant, called George, started stomping around the study, uprooting a surreal mix of trees and bookcases, typical of a dream world. Then this Judy Garland awoke not in Kansas but in Bishopthorpe and resumed reality.

The real Senior Staff I deeply love and respect. The oldest elephant is Donald Snelgrove, who retired as Bishop of Hull during this diary's year. He nobly ministered in the Hull area for over thirty years. As archdeacon, he inducted my father into a Hull living twenty years ago, and fondly remembers my sitting on his knee at the reception afterwards. Since I was eighteen at the time, I think (and hope) his memory is faulty here. My brother, eleven years my junior, was a far more likely and cuddly candidate.

Gordon Bates, the Bishop of Whitby, has the very best traits of a Yorkshireman. Abrupt, direct, with a dry wit, he is a strikingly successful preacher, decisive committee chairman, and loyal friend. I hardly ever think of him without thinking of his wife, Betty, for they often travel as a couple; a couple so normal and human that they win the hearts of all they encounter. Numberless clergy and people across the diocese have benefited from their natural care.

Humphrey Taylor, Bishop of Selby, is the master of both incisive phrase and action. I admire his being brave enough repeatedly to proclaim that the emperor has no clothes. I also admire his being unruffled by the barracking of those who like to fool themselves that the emperor is fully dressed. Unusually for a bishop he sports a black rather than a purple shirt, which led to a misunderstanding when I sent him his first ordinand to interview. Not having met the Bishop before, the ordinand assumed that the black-shirted gentleman who admitted him into the Bishop's house was either a chaplain or a visiting cleric. When the latter began intense questioning, the ordinand gave short reply, thinking, 'Who on earth does this busybody think he is interrogating?' Only after twenty minutes of celebrating a near Right to Silence did the truth dawn, too late to alter the appalling impression given. My diplomatic powers were stretched to the full to bring both men to revisit each other.

I need hardly introduce George Austin. Both my father and I served as vicars in his archdeaconry, and felt the pastoral care he displayed to clergy was superb, clearly the best we had ever encountered. Considering his uncompromising stand against homosexuality amongst the clergy, it comes as a surprise to find him married to someone named Bobbie. Reassuringly Bobbie is healthily and attractively female, a character in her own right. The hospitality they extend is warm, generous, and uncalculating. The fact that George and I are on opposite sides over 'the issue' both grieves me and makes me determined that those two sides should coexist. There would be a tremendous gap if he was not around.

Hugh Buckingham, Archdeacon of the East Riding, is a deeply spiritual man with an equally deep concern for person-hood and family life. He also is not afraid to be an irritant. Your response to him depends, I suppose, on whether you're a fellow irritant or a recipient of his irritation. He is a man without guile, without sycophancy, prepared to battle alone; I admire his integrity.

I am very fond of Chris Hawthorn because as a six-year-old I saw him ordained alongside my father, so I feel we go back a long way. A man of unflagging energy and financial acumen with a crisp turn of phrase, he proves an ideal Archdeacon of Cleveland, complete with eyes that twinkle whatever the time of day and to whatever depths of boredom any meeting plummets. And they do plummet; every time I leave a meeting of the Archbishop's Council, I can imagine only too well how Jesus must have felt when he was released from the tomb.

That completes the diocesan elephants. The diocesan fleas (amongst whom my dream cast me) warrant no description.

Today disaster strikes. A tooth abscess lays the Archbishop low in bed, which means the Senior Staff Meeting has to cope alone. It is no fun, since he is the chairman *par excellence*, with exactly the right level of humour, authority, and understanding to diffuse the most volatile situation. Without him the Senior Staff end up having a furious row over breast-feeding (a surprising topic for such an august body) and Forward (??) in Faith.

They are a funny lot, the Senior Staff. Though a lovable bunch their prayers always disappoint me. The meeting starts with a Eucharist, but they all hang around outside chapel until the very last moment, like relatives visiting an aged, malevolent aunt in an old people's home, going through the motions, wanting to keep the visit's time to an absolute minimum. Maybe some would steal into chapel earlier, but are bound by the rules of the hale and hearty pack.

Such a contrast to the Archbishop. John Habgood will be remembered for many things: Science and Religion; diplomacy; the Act of Synod; fidelity to the intellectual's quest to believe with integrity. And yet what I feel is his most abiding work remains chiefly hidden: his prayers. To hear him pray is a unique experience. His prayers reflect the attentiveness and alertness of an ever-patient God. The right words, the right phrases, the right pauses come so naturally, with not an ounce of the false piety which infests the prayers of others. His prayers have a glorious poetic ring to them, betraying an odour of sanctity.

Black Anglican Concerns in York Minster. More black faces in the congregation than usual (although the Minster has never been renowned for a multiracial presence), with a tanned look to the usual white faces, as if they have come out in sympathy. In lieu of a Gradual hymn, a slender Indian girl in native costume (complete with bells on her ankles) performs a dance of adoration. All very fetching, with a hint of eroticism; that the Christian God celebrates such things has hitherto been kept very well hidden.

This dance was highly successful. You need to be mindful, though, of the effect a dance designed to be viewed from a distance has on those in close proximity to the area of performance. One visit to a church in the Lake District included girls scantily clad in diaphanous material dancing under our very noses. One had to look interested, but not *that* interested. Had Wordsworth been there, I am sure he would have celebrated being surrounded by a host of golden nipples.

The Black Anglicans and York Minster proved a happy match. Bishop Wilfred Woods preached on Joseph being a paradigm for black Anglicans, hurt by their stronger (white) brothers, but ultimately the means of their salvation. A memorable sermon, not least for its revealed graffiti: 'To do is to be' (Descartes), 'Do-be-do-be-do' (Sinatra).

Returning in the car, the Archbishop vented his own humour. Drawing on the story of Joseph he observed that the butler was raised up whilst the baker was doomed. 'Just like the Butler Education Act and the Baker Education Act,' he quipped.

27 JULY

One undoubtable qualification for an archbishop is to keep a studied seriousness when all around you is quite clearly ridiculous. To be faced by a barrister with wig askew with the request, 'My Lord Archbishop, I bid leave to exhibit my proxy,' would cause lesser men to dissolve in paroxysms of mirth. But the Archbishop remained unmoved by a suggestiveness that harked back to the age of the music-hall.

The venue was not a music-hall, however, but a court in the bowels of York Minster to confirm the election of Michael Turnbull as Bishop of Durham. Archaic language abounded: the other forty million or so citizens of England (who for various reasons could not make the ceremony on this sultry July afternoon) are pronounced contumacious by the Archbishop. Perhaps a rather harsh judgement by a disciple of the man who welcomed all.

After convoluted legal proceedings the sentence is pronounced by the Archbishop as judge: Michael Turnbull is to be taken down and sentenced to reside in Auckland Castle for the rest of his working life. So help him God.

Tea in the cafeteria of St William's College is a much more jolly affair, although it is obviously disquieting for the other customers to be invaded by the ecclesiastical *crème de la crème*. Registrars, advocates, and bishops-elect sit side by side with tourists munching Eccles cakes.

3 AUGUST

On the third day there was a hundred-and-fiftieth anniversary in Tyne and Wear, so a near-dawn start to return to the Archbishop's former diocese of Durham. The one-and-a-half-hour journey, like all our journeys, was conducted in silence: Gordon the chauffeur driving, me beside him writing, the Archbishop writing and reading in the back. We both respect his need for a silence in which he can think, pray, and recharge in the midst of so many great pressures. Even so, this mute car hurtling through the land has an eeriness about it at times: the Word became flesh and said, 'Hush, be still.'

We go to a lot of centenaries, bicentenaries, tricentenaries, milleniums . . . The Archbishop has a favourite theme. Sketch the historical scene at the time the particular church was founded, emphasizing all the turmoil, the anxiety, the fears around then for the present and the future. Do not labour the point, but at some stage in the sermon compare all that *angst* with the present day, stressing how lucky we really are when our concerns are put into perspective by a far more grim past.

Only once did it fail to deliver, when he took it as read that some poor bedraggled inner-city congregation would naturally be watching 'the excellent serial *Martin Chuzzlewit* on BBC2.' *Eastenders* would have been too subtle for them, I fear.

Today proved a little different. Instead of the dreary ASB readings for a Dedication Festival we had those for Social Responsibility, which warmed my Bennite heart. The worship was well-ordered, began ten minutes early ('Everyone's here who's coming,' the incumbent reassured us) and the choir, made shrill by the high percentage of elderly ladies it contained, sang their hearts out. The Archbishop's sermon was animated, displaying a shrewd knowledge of the history of the place, with short sharp sentences making a clear message. Any church was a sign that life without God was stunted. It should offer the key to full life, especially for the marginalized and the young. (Was this a coded way of saying he liked 'Shine, Jesus, shine' I wondered?) Finally the church should offer redemption for the wrong turnings everyone makes in their life and live out acceptance of one another.

Abiding memories of the day? The servers, typically County Durham, dark-skinned, short cropped hair, broad necks, even in their childhood seemingly resigned to hardship. The magnificent view from the church perched on a hilltop across the Wear valley, even making the industrial wastes of Sunderland tolerable at such a distance on such a sunny day. The local lass, recently returned from a holiday in Kenya, the tight plaits in her hair (put there by a native) still as fixed as her sharp memory of the destitution, putting our petty destitutions into perspective. The drive back with the stunning Cleveland hills in the distance, filtered through the grime of industrial Teesside.

8 AUGUST

A routine day. Mail from the weekend to respond to, people to interview, speeches to write. Our studies are situated in the former roof of the chapel, which makes for a holy time if you dwell on eight centuries of archiepiscopal prayer trapped in the rafters. It also makes for a very warm time indeed in this continuing high summer. Mid-afternoon I offer to buy the Archbishop an ice-cream to keep us cool; he declines with an amused and pitying look which makes me wonder whether I have breached some protocol. Or perhaps archbishops are blessed with cooling systems which are denied inferior clergy.

John Habgood is one of the most self-contained characters around: socially and intellectually he is self-sufficient. This might make lesser mortals ideal candidates for a desert island, since, after all, what need have they of any others? John Habgood is bigger than that. By no means a recluse, from a secure base he reaches out to others through sheer interest in them and love of them. Because that base is secure, there seems to be a remarkable lack of calculation in his relationships, no 'What can I get out of this?' or 'What can this person do for me?' This is an unusual, though not unique quality: after all, God's eternal activity is to reach out, not from necessity but from sheer love.

Self-sufficiency can have its unusual facets, though. We often both work in our studies of an evening, and from time to time the Archbishop, contained in his own world, will forget that I am around. The most memorable occasion was when I was in the filing room, saw him breeze past the door and wished him good night. His sole reply was to flick off all the lights.

As I fumbled along the dark passageway searching for unfamiliar switches I found one fire door particularly resistant. I pushed and pushed to no avail. In the end I gave up and felt along the wall until I found the elusive switch.

All was then revealed. Instead of pushing a door I had been putting my weight on a large glass-fronted photograph, depicting the 1958 Lambeth Conference of Bishops. This was the conference which the then Archbishop of Canterbury concluded with the magisterial words 'Class dismissed'; he clearly did not see the Anglican Communion as a collaborative exercise! Strangely the conference had given a guarded OK to contraception (at least for Anglicans). I have never seen a group of men who looked less likely candidates to discuss such delicate matters. Formally dressed, severe, headmasterly, puritanical, their frozen faces all stared implacably at the camera, looking furious at my attempted intrusion into their world, undisturbed for thirty-seven years. I thanked God with all my heart that I worked for a human being and not one of these male gorgons.

A Harvest Festival in the deep country, so deep that there are sheep grazing in the churchyard. From time to time we get letters of complaint about such things along the lines of

> Dear Archbishop,
>
> I was going to my auntie's grave as I am wont to do every alternate Michaelmas. I was thoroughly disgusted to find sheep in the graveyard eating the flowers and defecating (not always the word used) everywhere . . .

Actually sheep are a jolly effective way of keeping churchyard grass down. At our harvest church they were fenced in to stop them straying onto recent graves and devouring flowers, thereby lightening our postbag. 'It's an electric fence which keeps them in,' the vicar told us proudly.

'It can't be,' the Archbishop retorted. 'Those rope strands could never conduct electricity.' He practised what he preached by clutching the fence between finger and thumb. I held my breath, but there were no blue flashes and my Archbishop did not disappear in a puff of smoke. However, the vicar did point out the humming transformer with the cathode and anode firmly clipped to the fence netting.

Lest the Archbishop be thought superhuman, I quickly pointed out his rubber-soled shoes (standard wear for Primates), explaining that these had insulated him and stopped the current going to earth. Should he have returned barefoot in the early morning dew, then he might not have been so lucky. But the whole episode was an interesting example of how, if John Habgood decided something shouldn't work then it wouldn't work. *Vox archiepiscopi, vox dei.*

The little church was a gem. Round Early Norman dogtooth arches popped up everywhere: in the porch, beneath the tower, spanning a wide chancel; the latter encased in plaster, the result of ill-intentioned Victorian decoration. The place was like old Covent Garden on vegans' day, saturated with lush fruit and vegetables. A tractor rear tyre, whose hub diameter fortunately matched that of the ancient font, had been hooped over the base and supported a pyramid of produce. A delicate arrangement of bread and grapes with a eucharistic theme festooned the altar; I placed the Archbishop's crosier thereon very timidly, just in case the whole arrangement should come tumbling down, with grapes rolling down the aisle like marbles.

One of the choristers rang the three bells with the aid of an intriguing pulley system. I never realized you could get so many tunes off three notes, whilst wondering at the appropriateness of 'Down at the old Bull and Bush' as a fitting invitation to Evensong. Applications for the post of churchwarden in this little village were obviously restricted to graduates only, since both wardens proudly wore gowns and hoods.

The service was according to the Book of Common Prayer; the language seemed entirely right and natural for this congregation who so easily could have spanned the centuries. The lessons were read well, with typically slow and thoughtful Yorkshire intonation. In the Old Testament Lesson from Exodus 'wandering Aramaean' was read as 'wandering Armenian', an understatement indeed if he was so far off course as to end up in Palestine.

The Archbishop preached on receiving and giving. He had once been delayed in Leicester and had engaged a native in conversation about local traits. 'Folk in Leicester don't give and receive, they lose and get,' was his sour summary.

'Are we a giving and receiving society or a getting and losing society?' was the Archbishop's poser for our rustic congregation.

He developed his theme well. At a party he had once come across the chief cashier of the Bank of England, whose job it was to sign the banknotes. He asked him the question which he had stored up for a lifetime: 'If I gave you a banknote with your signature to the promise to pay the bearer on demand the sum of £5, what would you give me?'

'Another note,' the cashier replied, wearied I guess by everyone he encountered posing this chestnut. But the Archbishop found the response shattering since it revealed the framework of utter trust that undergirds any monetary system. For a society to survive and work, we have to accept the worth of one another's labour on trust.

The Archbishop told his enthralled congregation how he disliked the phrase 'taxpayers' money' since it assumed a false air of benevolence on the part of the taxpayer, as if he were graciously funding society. If society did not exist, then taxpayers would not have any money for anything. Taxes were the *sine qua non* support for the system which generated the wealth.

Which is precisely where God came in. Without taxes, no society. Without God, no world. Harvest was not just a thanksgiving for pretty flowers and tasty potatoes, with a nod towards God's direction for his minimal assistance. It is nothing less than a primeval acknowledgement that the whole of our order derived from God, an offering of the earth's fruits to the very source from which they came.

It was a striking sermon in its ingenuity, and rose way above the usual tedious and sentimental harvest fare. 'What sort of person you are is revealed by how you use your money' was a message which struck home; getters and losers slept ill in their beds that night.

Our venue: a delightful but tiny moors village, overcast by a pall of smoke from stubble burning. We were greeted by a rural dean more nervous than usual and a new incumbent less nervous than he should have been. The church was pretty and full, with a geriatric organist whose gnarled fingers moved painfully and lovingly over an ancient organ. Equally geriatric clergy huddled together in the choir stalls to support their new colleague. A twinkly-eyed archdeacon completed the pack.

The Archbishop was at ease and held the whole congregation—even a man fainting in the middle of his talk didn't distract him—'Let him go out. The church is unusually hot and I guess unusually full . . .' To get a stiff-necked moorland congregation to smile is quite a feat; the Archbishop made them laugh.

The theme of the sermon was about a dig in Palestine which had revealed the remains of a fishing boat from Jesus' time with a dozen or so seats. Like those disciples, we were in the same boat, needing to row together in time and harmony to achieve any direction whatsoever. This theological version of the 'Eton Boat Song' pleased the locals, hopefully enough to tempt them out of their three separate religious ghettos, three villages, three churches which 'believed in the same God—at least some of the time.'

Perhaps the new incumbent's nerves were latent rather than absent. Following the sermon he invited us to a period of silent prayer which lasted all of five seconds. At the end of the service he wandered off, oblivious to the fact that he had to greet his flock. An archbishop affects people in all sorts of funny ways.

11 SEPTEMBER

To get caught up in a vintage car rally is unfortunate; to also get enmeshed in a cycle race seems positively careless. Our journey over the Pennines was one of stops and starts, the car soon reeking of the lethal fumes its ancestors pothered out as they chugged ahead. And when we were not choking, we had cycles blocking our path, swaying from side to side as their riders struggled with the incline.

Few people must rejoice when they see Burnley in their sights. We did, however, since it marked the end of our tedious journey. We crawled through the terraced streets—shades of *Open All Hours*—and eventually found the tiny little church whose anniversary we had come to celebrate. And it was tiny. Processions were difficult since you had no real need to process anywhere; stand up and take one pace and you were there. One step from the altar and you were in the pulpit; one step from the pulpit and you were before the plaque marking the Archbishop's visit, a veritable Gulliver in this house of Lilliput.

The sermon was a variation on the theme of the-turbulence-of-the-past-putting-the-turbulence-of-the-present-into-perspective variety and went down well. I am often being told that people on the other side of the Pennines are more God-fearing, but today I believed it. The hymn-singing was lusty, the prayer devout. Their vicar of twenty-five years was clearly much loved, his ministry much appreciated and repaid by so many, generation upon generation, coming to deeply held faith. He had been one of John Habgood's students at theological college. Without a doubt he had done his job well.

Devoted ladies of the parish served a delicious lunch which fortified us well for the long return journey, to be hoped to be unaccompanied by vintage cars and cycles. With great delight the vicar handed me an old photograph, holding the print almost with the reverence one would reserve for Scripture. A youthful John Habgood beamed out at me: owl-like spectacles, a cricket cap, flannels and pads, a bat in hand. He had been in the team playing against Westcott's neighbour, Jesus College. It must be the only time in the Archbishop's ministry that he had batted against Jesus.

The church looked so different from that sorry picture it had presented two years before: then it was little more than a burnt-out shell, gutted by a fire which was started deliberately.

But things were different today. The restored St Stephen's, Acomb, was to be re-dedicated with all pomp and splendour. We even put the archiepiscopal flag on the car, although the prime reason for this was to ensure a swift passage through a York thronging with Saturday afternoon shoppers. It had the desired effect: heads turned, normally surly lorry drivers gave way and we arrived in record time.

The redesigned church was truly splendid. Tastefully decorated, the chancel (cluttered with furniture before the fire) was now a pleasing open space, with the organ gallery imaginatively transformed into children's rooms, fronted with soundproof glass, where children could be seen and not heard. More importantly the children had a panoramic vantage point which held them enthralled. Perhaps the most striking feature was the high altar which had been severely charred by the flames and lovingly restored; shades of the Easter Jesus, resurrected but still definitely bearing the scars.

The Archbishop was at his very best, relaxed, completely with the folk there. He took his text from Ezra, where the former temple at Jerusalem had been restored following the Exile. Clearly there were mixed emotions around at that time, thrill at the restoration, sorrow for the original loss, so that during the celebrations the people could not distinguish the shout of joy from that of the weeping and wailing. 'Today we have been more restrained,' the Archbishop quipped.

But he clearly understood the loss that some would feel, those who sensed the new was not as good as the old, and wept and wailed in the silence of their hearts. He did not belittle this emotion. But he also pointed to the new features which were worthy of being marked with joy. He paralleled the whole experience with crucifixion and resurrection, not so much triumph following tragedy but triumph being forged in the very tragedy itself, so that weeping and joy were all mixed up. 'You have not only heard this gospel, you have now lived it, as you live it every day.'

Following the sermon the much-noted restraint took a nosedive as pent-up children were released from their gallery room, led with due indecorum by a dancing and streamer-waving lady. Guitars played, choruses were sung, the vicar clapped for sheer joy, the whole place became alive. Everyone was thrilled. Or should I say nearly everyone. One disgruntled old gent shuffled out down the aisle in protest, only to find himself caught up with the singing children as they beat a retreat to their lofty den.

On the bumpy road back (there has been an epidemic of sleeping policemen in York) the Archbishop pointed out a shady-looking establishment. 'David, have you tried there?' he asked kindly.

'No,' I replied, 'But I'm fond of Chinese take-aways, provided they don't get too shaken up on this road.'

'Oh, we usually eat on the premises,' the Archbishop rejoindered. Now that was a mind-blowing picture. Patrician Archbishop in a sly corner of a downtown Chinese restaurant. Still, it fitted with the day's sweet and sour theme.

Wherever we are going, it helps if we have a map. But even so, such maps are not always of use. For instance, often the well-meaning host will send a sketch where roundabouts are omitted or invented, or will refer to local landmarks 'which cannot be missed' (always a dangerous phrase) leaving us to find out as we wander aimlessly that they have been demolished years before.

Also, since I suffer from acute motion sickness, by the end of the journey I am not the world's best navigator. Positively the worst occasion was when we were booked in at Bury for a Church Urban Fund service one dark autumn evening. Already delayed on the Leeds ringroad, we speeded into Bury at one hundred miles an hour, not the best speed for a carsick chaplain to note the next turning. The result was that we ended up in Bury town centre (a wildly exciting place), irretrievably lost, with the minutes ticking away. I was all for having a Chinese take-away, going home and calling it a day, but the Archbishop persevered with grim determination. We retraced our steps and eventually found our church, only twenty minutes late.

For today's Confirmation at Market Weighton we had directions from none less than the Venerable Bede, venerable indeed since he wrote his unequalled church history over twelve hundred years ago. Our goal, to paraphrase Bede, was not far east of York, beyond the Derwent and (the sister church of) the place known as Goodmanham. In 627, Goodmanham was the site where Coifi the pagan high priest, aided and abetted by King Edwin and Paulinus, first Bishop of York, had torn down the pagan temples, shrines, and altars in favour of Christianity.

I was grateful to Bede for some of the best directions we had had for some time. We arrived in sleepy Market Weighton, with its intriguing brick church tower on a stone base, well ahead of time. But judging by the cross looks on some of the locals' faces, I wondered if the indigenous population had ever forgiven 'that lot from York' (as we are often affectionately known) for this act of gross vandalism, perpetuated just 1,350 years previously, a mere twinkling of an eye in Vale-of-York-time. The Archbishop was uncowed, however, and preached a truly brilliant sermon, setting the poser, 'What is the opposite of faith?'

'Doubt' was soon ruled out as a contender, since faith itself was forged in the flames of doubt, so was hardly an opposite. But 'works' certainly fitted the bill. Those who felt that Christianity was about perfection, living a set of rules, and working your way into heaven neglected the fact that God accepted us as we are, broadcasting that acceptance in the life of Jesus, with his love as a free gift, graciously given, and only devalued if attempted to be bought or earned. The final opposite was 'fear', which spoke at several levels. There was the fear of committing oneself to Christianity, with all the responsibilities that that would entail. There was also the fear of what lay ahead. Faith, however, countered that fear in that it emphasized God's presence with us throughout, willing us to get through it all, empowering us to survive in situations we would never dare tackle without him.

It was a Confirmation sermon *par excellence*, addressed directly to the candidates but with plenty of spin-offs for the congregation. I think our visit had been as momentous as Coifi's, but hopefully more constructive. At least by the end of the sermon, everyone looked less cross.

AUTUMN

22 SEPTEMBER

The Archbishop and I are not always together; sometimes the archiepiscopal road show splits and we go our separate ways. Ordinations are one example. In the early eighties, when I was ordained, numbers coming up for deaconing and priesting were so low that we could all be squeezed into Bishopthorpe Palace for the ninety-six-hour retreat beforehand—even if that did mean four of us to a bedroom and twice as many as that using the archiepiscopal bathroom. I recall succumbing to temptation before my priesting and using Mrs Archbishop's hair conditioner to heighten my good looks; unfortunately it had the opposite effect and my greasy hair had a rat tail look about it. No wonder the Archbishop gave me a funny stare when he laid hands on my oily head.

In order to prevent unseemly use of Mrs Archbishop's hair conditioner, and also because numbers at York ordinations have gone up in recent years (contrary to media hype), we now spend the first two days of the retreat at a more spacious place, with only the final hours cramped into Bishopthorpe.

So on the Thursday before the two annual ordinations I wave the Archbishop goodbye and take the ordinands deep into the country. In September our venue is Sleights, near Whitby, where the Retreat House is run by devoted nuns of the Order of the Holy Paraclete (not a rare breed of parrot but a synonym for the Spirit). I have known these nuns since I was a boy of six, when my parents used to take me on parish retreats. As a bouncy and chatty six-year-old I was, to say the least, bewildered by all these adults not talking to each other, as if they had had some almighty row. I realise now it was all preparation for working with a silent boss.

But the nuns took pity on me, and used to show me round the grounds, in the autumn encouraging me to rustle through the deep-pile carpet of golden leaves. I must be one of the few clergymen in the Church of England who was taught to play conkers by a nun!

In those days the Retreat House they ran was more isolated, at the south-eastern end of the North York Moors. In my memory we always ate fish: poached fish, grilled fish, fried fish, fish pie, the permutations seemed endless. By the end of the retreat I was invariably sick; certainly ever since I have had a distinct aversion to fish. When our Lord (in Luke's Gospel) eats broiled fish following his resurrection, this definitely seems to me one of the lesser attractions of the afterlife. As I am sure St Paul said somewhere, 'If for fish only we hope, we of all men are most to be pitied.'

The fish stopped. Tragically, because the fish delivery man was caught in the snow drifts of 1963's fierce winter on his way to the isolated Retreat House, and froze to death. The nuns' cuisine had to be more versatile after that (despite the windfall of frozen fish); understandably another fish man could not be persuaded to serve the fatal route.

All that was a long, long time ago. Though the food has changed, the nuns remain the same, a constancy which offers some comfort for a chaplain separated from his archbishop.

24 SEPTEMBER

Not that we are apart for long; Saturday afternoon brings us together again with a convoy of ordinands in tow. Ordinands' reactions vary to being in the presence of the Archbishop in his country seat. Most are overawed and are struck silent; some enthuse and giggle and talk too much; I am constantly surprised by how few of the men wear a smart suit. The most natural in recent years was a delightful Australian who was simply himself. Who else would dare look at the Archbishop's prize border terriers and say to him, 'Gee, what strange-looking dogs; are they some sort of breed or just mongrels?'

He maintained the canine theme during dinner in the lower dining-room, bringing the meal to a halt with his exclamation, 'One of those dogs has snatched my serviette.'

Archbishop and Mrs Habgood were quickly on their knees, crawling under the table, trying to flush the offending hound out. 'Well, he's never done this before. How extraordinary!' said Mrs Habgood, apologetically.

The search was ended as abruptly as it had begun, with an outburst from our Antipodean friend, 'Strewth! The dog never stole it after all. I've gone and stuffed it in my pocket, thinking it was my hankie.' The whole party dusted themselves down and the meal resumed, with the Archbishop managing to look as if search parties for dogs with errant serviettes were part and parcel of his everyday existence.

The last word deservedly goes to our Australian. As we drove to the rehearsal, the Archbishop at the wheel (Gordon, the driver, plays Bridge on Saturday night), the soaring towers of the Minster drawing nearer in the dusk, an Aussie voice chirped up from the back of the car, 'Gee, this is really bizarre!'

He was profoundly right. Although playing conkers with fish-eating nuns at an early age gives one a little immunity to bizarreness, it is hardly enough to cover the bizarre situations encountered as John Habgood's chaplain.

29 SEPTEMBER

On Michaelmas morn I drove to the Minster to rehearse the new Dean's installation, to take place later that afternoon. I mused that the best collective noun for a group of canons was a confusion, as we all muddled through, processing to every corner of the Minster. The Chapter Clerk, a retired army man, clearly saw the whole exercise as a military manoeuvre, but I am afraid the conscripts were unruly and would have won no wars.

As always, it was all right on the night. The confusion of canons gathering in a dark side aisle before the service looked as subversive and conspiratorial a group as one could ever encounter. The two legal officers in attendance were having an animated discussion about the latest legal fashions. Length of wigs and numbers of buttons on waistcoats were talked of as earnestly as a father agonizing over his errant daughter's skirt lengths. In the midst of all this preparation was the Archbishop, standing tall and silent, taking it all in, his eyes blinking like a wise owl. Another striking figure was Ray Furnell, the new Dean, relaxed with a warmth which was immense and immediate.

Our first port of call was the ancient Chapter House; as is customary I led the Archbishop with the heavy primatial cross. When our Lord urged his disciples to take up their cross, I do not feel this bejewelled specimen was quite what he had in mind. I teased the Archbishop that he ought to name me Simon of Cyrene because of my load; 'You'll always carry a cross,' he quipped chillingly.

The secrecy and strangeness of dealings in the Chapter House was quasi-masonic, with whispering canons in a circle, each seated in their own alcove recessed into the Chapter House wall. The Chancellor somewhat curiously (but strictly according to tradition) marked the Dean's welcome by presenting him with a book, a bread bun (to chew if he was bored with the book perhaps) and a kiss. Actually the kiss did not even achieve the status of a peck. Obviously allegations of senior churchmen's sexual preferences had taken their toll.

Next came an invigorating walk to the Choir where the new Dean was installed. The curtains to the Nave were drawn so that the canons, bishops, and other peculiar clergy could don their copes. The whole thing smacked of some overcrowded ecclesiastical boutique. Tall canons with short copes swapped with small canons with long copes and then the curtains were swished back and York Minster's 1994 autumn collection was unleashed on the nave catwalk. Very fetching they all looked too; and all immensely dramatic.

Red-cassocked Minster choir integrated with maroon-cassocked St Edmundsbury choir in aural if not visual harmony. Parry's setting of Psalm 122 was memorable indeed, not least for the wild and enthusiastic gesticulations of the choirmaster.

The Dean was duly licensed. The Archbishop preached 'a truly brilliant sermon' in the words of his wife, although in my experience, wives tend to be biased. Even so, it was brilliant. 'The Dean has been inducted, installed, prayed over, licensed; in fact, there's not much more you can do to a man . . .' The congregation roared. The Archbishop then followed the humour with a message that was clear and uncompromising. The Minster was a ladder to heaven (York and Jacob can sound remarkably similar, especially in Hebrew), soaring the spirits of all pilgrims from both near and far. But the Minster also had to be a ladder from heaven if it was ever to be really effective, allowing its founder to 'come down' and dwell in its midst. That indwelling was marked by worship and prayer, and on the subject of worship there was to be no sloppiness or second-rateness. I noticed some of the senior clergy were shivering, despite the warm autumn day.

Preaching, in particular, was to be exemplary. The Arch-bishop recalled how the priest–poet, John Donne, had preached for more than two hours at St Paul's only to have his concluding remarks greeted with shouts of 'More, more,' from an enthusiastic congregation. Two centuries on, people still appreciated sermons of quality. 'But since I don't hear shouts of "More, more", I feel I have given the new Dean sufficient to think about . . .' And so he closed.

The Dean read the prayers very effectively, punctuating the set text with a moment's prayer for the car ferry, *Estonia*, lost at sea. As one woman (who shall be nameless) said afterwards, 'His voice is the sort that makes a woman swoon. I just had to give him a kiss to make him feel welcome.' Presumably a kiss of consolation to compensate for the Chancellor's reticence.

The day had been sheer thrill. I have a deep-rooted and long-standing love for the Minster. My affair with it began when, as a very bewildered six-year-old, I had watched my father ordained there. In the same place twenty years later, and only a little less bewildered, I too was ordained. For me it is a very good place to be, whatever. Doubly good when undoubted quality of venue is matched by quality of event, as it was this Michaelmas Day.

1 OCTOBER

To Beverley for the Bishop of Hull's farewell, the final one. Our last trip to the Minster there had been for a confirmation, a service whose formality had contrasted with the lightness of touch that that place now has. The coffee table look-alike altar and the vivid banners hanging from nearly every pillar instill a warmth and relaxed feel into what could be a very cold building; I certainly remember being chilled there in my boyhood.

But formality seldom goes right. Things started going wrong when I realized I had packed the wrong colours. We had red, everyone else was in white. Rather than looking like the Manchester United reserves, I reversed my stole to gold (a fortunate colour for a lining) and the Archbishop went stoleless. 'No one will notice,' he shrugged. There was a hint of recrimination there which has made me pack every possible colour since. Sometimes we look like an itinerant ecclesiastical outfitters.

However my impasse was nothing compared to the mistake of the night. Two of the forty or so candidates had to be baptized as well as confirmed, so at the appropriate moment we duly processed to the font. What a procession! Crucifer, acolytes, choir, clergy, candidates, vergers, the lot. The crucifer was exceedingly keen and set off five minutes earlier than he should have done, so was called back for his false start—perhaps introducing drugs tests for crucifers wouldn't be a bad idea! But eventually we got off, and after a brisk and lengthy walk to the other side of the vast building we arrived at the ancient font. The Archbishop, with due decorum, mounted the steps and peered into an empty bowl: 'There's no water!' he exclaimed.

The vicar rubbed his brow in desperation and despatched a verger to some nether recess. The minutes ticked by. The Archbishop began adlibbing about how precious water is in the Third World, where people are used to carrying it miles. But even he dried up as we realized tonight's carrier was enduring a similar distance. We waited and waited until after what seemed an age our Aquarius-in-black returned—with a red fire bucket. Its contents were duly tipped into the font. I guess the bucket usually stored sand, since there were big coagulated lumps floating on the water's surface. The Archbishop nonchalantly resumed with no further hitches.

Maybe all baptisms are doomed to go wrong. The story goes that the aged St Patrick, baptizing a chieftain in an Irish river, accidentally impaled the chieftain's foot with the sharpened end of his crosier, on which he was wont to lean. It was only after the baptism was over that Patrick noticed the blood spurting everywhere. His apologies were profuse.

Never had baptism been so efficacious, because the warlike chieftain was easily placated. 'You see,' he informed the saint, 'First I thought of the pains our Lord went through on my behalf, and how trivial my own pains were in comparison. And secondly, never having been baptized before, I thought it was all part of the ceremony!'

I just hope that those two baptized that night with water and with sand assumed it was all part of the ceremony too . . .

At the Bishop of Hull's farewell, no one stood on ceremony. Donald Snelgrove preached his last sermon as Hull's bishop genuinely, movingly, and effectively, focusing on his ministry as reconciler. With great sadness he mentioned those who were conspicuous by their absence from this farewell, who placed themselves out of communion with him because he had ordained women as priests. Much has been made of their hurt, but I felt hurt for him in the twilight of his ministry spurned by those he had thought friends. With only months left of his episcopate, he had taken the first women's ordination in York Minster, not because he had to, but because he had felt it profoundly right. To write off someone's long and rich ministry because of that act of principle seemed a great shame. With great pride the Bishop had shown the Archbishop the colour photograph the *Hull Daily Mail* had presented him with, depicting that ordination. He was rightly proud.

Apart from that real sadness, the farewell was a great celebration. The Bishop movingly talked of those he had seen grow up in his thirty-odd years, the steward who served his coffee on the London train who had been his first confirmation candidate, the judge who had been in his youth club (and probably not such a tearaway in those far-off days). Afterwards he was presented with a cheque, a picture, and a chair whose magnificent bulk matched his. As the chair was being carried to the stage, it came to pieces in the vicar's hands, so was hastily reassembled. Then the delighted Bishop duly sat on his prize.

Unfortunately the chair's reassembly had been of necessity hasty and unfortunately therefore incomplete. I held my breath as it threatened to tip its episcopal contents over the back of the stage right onto the grave of the good St John, revered local saint and archbishop. But the unthinkable did not happen, the tributes poured back and forth and brought out Donald and Sylvia Snelgrove's sheer sense of fun and devotion to each other. Beverley Minster at its informal best.

To *the* Minster to preach on William Tyndale's five-hundredth anniversary. Who? The Archbishop answered that question in the opening paragraphs of his sermon, as he rattled off memorable texts from the Authorized Version of the Bible which had their origin in Tyndale's bold translation. He also mentioned some that had not been retained, such as the serpent in Genesis 3 saying to Eve, 'Tush, you shall not die.'

'It's a pity they didn't keep that; "Tush" seems a very snakelike word to me,' the Archbishop remarked, with a smile on his face.

Another sad omission in Genesis' later chapters is 'God was with Joseph and he was a lucky fellow,' to be replaced with the Authorized Version's rather milder, 'God was with Joseph and he prospered.' Tyndale captured the essence of Incarnation here.

Tyndale was clearly the right man for the right moment. Before him translations had been too literal and therefore obscure. Modern translations were necessarily pedestrian for a pedestrian society, but lacked the resonances of Tyndale's magisterial text, which had shaped the very language we enjoy. Religious expression needed poetry *à la* Tyndale; without it is 'like crumpets without butter'. At this point in the sermon the Archbishop realized he had lapsed into pedestrianism himself, so scratched around for a more poetic phrase. 'Like birds without wings,' he substituted. Since we were having chicken for dinner, this phrase didn't strike me as particularly poetic either. I would have said, 'like eyes without sparkle'. But there again, I do not write his sermons. If I did, as a fan of New Testament textual transmission, I would have been more cautious in my remarks about Erasmus.

Erasmus aside, it was a remarkable sermon, instilling a thirst for Tyndale's words; and what better effect could a sermon have than to drive you to Scripture?

The new Dean took up the theme, masterly praying for 'those who write what many read and speak what many hear'. The voice which made women swoon had a more gravelly tone as he succumbed to a typical Vale of York cold.

The communion was from the Book of Common Prayer, hardly my wife's favourite. The Archbishop took up the subject with her, arguing that the old Prayer Book had its good points, still harking on his religion-needing-poetry theme. Rachel responded well (most people are shocked into silence in the Archbishop's presence), saying that she had enjoyed coming to the Minster that morning since it had been worthwhile for the history lesson.

Joking apart, I fear many clergy feel betrayed over this subject. Encouraged by their superiors to accept and promote revision of services as not just new translations but also recovery of the practice of the Early Church, they then hear the same superiors extolling the virtues of the old order. I guess the dearth of the poetic turn of phrase in modern services had driven the hierarchy to revisit the BCP. In addition, I am afraid the latest scholarship indicates that worship of the Early Church was actually very diverse, with the presumed uniform practice so needed to fire liturgical revision elusive. No longer can any scholar say with certainty, 'This is what the Early Church did, let's copy them.'

It seems ironic then that John Habgood, architect of the Alternative Service Book, should be such a fan of the Book of Common Prayer. Or perhaps he runs true to the paradox which is essentially him. At the end of the day, people brought up on the BCP need and deserve resonances with their past. But those not brought up on it need other resonances. My three small daughters, who nightly say the modern version of the Lord's Prayer need to see that featured in their Sunday worship; a need which York Minster on the eighteenth Sunday after Trinity failed abysmally to address.

6 OCTOBER

Happy Birthday to you! Three score years and ten and five might be a venerable age for an adult, but for a hobbit and a diocese still virtual babyhood. Even so, it is good to go to a baby's birthday, so we snaked to Bradford to enjoy the diocesan party, Gordon choosing the windiest route to put us off our jellies and sandwiches. The birthday cake was an octagon, with a side for each bishop since 1919. The Archbishop and present Bishop had to pose endlessly for the Press, cutting and recutting the cake's first slice. The poses they were forced into made them look like models for a clerical outfitter's catalogue—'Special offer this month: buy three worsted suits and get a pectoral cross free!'

The party was splendid. Tea as it would have been served in 1919 (they must have turned the fridge up to keep it so fresh) with visitors that spanned the Diocese's links across the world as well as its short history. David Blunt was there, whose father, Bishop Blunt, had preached a sermon that indirectly caused an abdication. And they dare to say no one listens to sermons these days.

The celebration transferred from Bishop's House to Cathedral with processions galore. The service was one which had several false starts, including a lengthy but largely incomprehensible greeting from the Bishop of Sudan; even so it was good to see our persecuted brother in Christ who has been so much held in our prayers.

The Archbishop in his sermon ran a *tour de force* through the famous names that had dominated Bradford's last seventy-five years and congratulated the baby diocese on its unstuffiness. I am afraid that by the end of the evening stuffiness became a positive attraction as the Diocese demonstrated only too well that it had moved from babyhood to adolescence. 'We are marching in the light of Christ' drew the whole congregation into a writhing dance, with the honourable exception of the Bishops of Southwark and Kingston, the Archbishop and me. My advice to the Archbishop was to dive for cover under the nearby High Altar if things got any hotter.

No charismatic ditty would be complete without dancing girls, who cavorted in the aisles, streamers and all. They seemed to be using the aforesaid streamers to whip the cathedral floor for some misdemeanour. I am sure there was some deep theological significance lurking there, but I am afraid it was lost on me. I wondered if Miss Whiplashes the world over realized the profound religious symbolism of their acts; perhaps that very numinous appeal goes a long way to explain their tremendous popularity.

Predictably, the service closed with 'Shine, Jesus, shine' with encore after encore. A former Bishop of the adolescent Diocese, but now Bishop of a very grown-up diocese, mouthed an aside at me: 'This is the seventh time I've sung this thing in seven days and I'm fed up!'

All told, an enjoyable day with some lively welcoming people. Whatever the Diocese of Bradford becomes when it grows up, I hope it does not lose its exuberance.

13 OCTOBER

To St Aidan's, Leeds, for their centenary. A massive church with a massive mural on the apse predictably depicting Aidan and all his works. At least Aidan looks more lifelike than his statue on Holy Island, where he seems to be eating a mega-cornetto (actually the flame of the gospel).

The architecture of St Aidan's is Romanesque on a grand scale, with rounded arches at every turn, raised baptistry, altar, and pulpit, all on exactly the same level, since Sacrament and Word are equals in the C of E. At St Aidan's, Sacrament is more equal than others. For our visit there was a display of ornate vestments, curiously set alongside the carnival queen's dress; I was glad that the Archbishop did not have to model it. The thurifer was the most vigorous I had ever seen, thrusting his thurible like a Scottish hurler, with wafts of incense billowing up to the lofty rafters. He was accompanied by a sweet Afro-Caribbean boatgirl with tight locks and innocent smile. The choir was large and vivacious, with clearly a strong musical tradition dominating the place. Given that, the Mass setting was rather curious, resonant of the theme tune of *Dr Finlay's Casebook*; perhaps it was all to match our Scottish hurler.

The Archbishop presided in the old sense of the word, preaching, absolving, and blessing, but leaving the rest to everyone else. The vicar celebrated, with fellow staff and venerable former incumbents concelebrating Communion around him, whispering the words together in quite an effective way which illustrated the continuing ministry over the decades.

The Archbishop's sermon was on 'living stones'. He reassured the congregation of his knowledge of the place by mentioning his son, a Leeds policeman, and his daughter, at one time a doctor in the casualty department at 'Jimmy's' down the road. Both had encountered the results of 'domestics' which were apparently prevalent in Chapeltown. In broad brush strokes he painted an accurate picture of the area, not making it out to be what it was not, but simply noting the roughness, the racial mix—a veritable melting-pot, yet with opportunities for integration, to which St Aidan's congregation bore eloquent witness.

A service in Leeds city, in a parish with a sizeable proportion of Barbados situated within it, attended inexplicably by the Lord Mayor of Birmingham naturally demanded that the Archbishop should preach about Liverpool Cathedral. Another massive building, its glory was that it conveyed a wholeness despite being composed of countless individual sandstones, of all sizes, each in its allotted place. The curious thing about sandstone was that it had to be set the same way up as it occurred naturally, otherwise it rapidly deteriorated.

Obvious lessons to be learnt. A group of Christians, though like the Liverpool stones all different shapes and sizes (you're telling me!), could achieve a marvellous wholeness. And both the attraction and the essence of Christianity was that people didn't have to pretend to be what they were not. God could use them in their natural state; indeed they had to be the people they were meant to be, without illusion. Only then could God be effective through them.

Interestingly, the architect of Liverpool Cathedral humbly put his signature on the smallest stone, mirroring the activity of God, who puts his name to the least in his mission to affirm the ordinary. Just as ordinary bread and wine can have the taste of God about them, we ordinary men and women can be stones which live for him.

An uplifting sermon for a community in many ways on the edge of today's society. As we disrobed in the church hall, I stood the silver primatial cross by a mop. Truly affirming the ordinary. Mind you, I made sure Gordon did not confuse the two when packing. Even an Archbishop who consistently affirmed the ordinary would not be best pleased to be preceded by a squeegee at his next appointment.

16 OCTOBER

I did not go with him to Jedburgh. I nearly did, since his tooth abscess reoccurred and I offered to do the driving. But he recovered sufficiently and opted to go alone; after all, since he is capable of running the Church of England, he is capable of driving to Jedburgh.

I had this funny feeling that he always wanted to make the visit on his own anyway. At first I thought it was all to do with his not wanting to return to the place where he was Rector thirty years before as the conquering hero, complete with peaked-capped chauffeur and primatial-crossed chaplain. But then I realized that I had read him wrong, that he was simply not bothered by all the archiepiscopal trimmings, neither taking pride in them nor being embarrassed by them.

Yet I still had this sense that this was a personal pilgrimage into his past which he had to make by himself. And so I had to be content with accompanying him in spirit.

The journey would be like a time line. First the drive past Durham Cathedral, towers soaring above the autumn mist that even a day's sun had been unable to conquer. Would he recall a 46-year-old man, with a babe still in arms, suddenly the master of Auckland Castle in the steps of the Prince Bishops, Lightfoot, Westcott, Ramsey . . . ? Some are born great, some achieve greatness, and some have greatness thrust upon them. John Habgood's greatness visited him in all three guises.

The drive crosses the Tyne and wends north-west into North-umberland, the protection of Hadrian's wall soon left far behind to the south. Border country invaded by John Habgood, no stranger to the world of the frontier in either theology or faith. Beyond the frontiers population reduces, the traffic thins out, settlements are fewer and further between. The many forests of Northumberland with the Kielder forest to the west catch the eye, their deciduous trees with golden leaves of various hue, their autumn resonating with John Habgood's autumn, the autumn of his ministry.

Hills rise to the north-east, the Cheviot the queen of them all, terrible in their majesty and mystery, yet still with a hint of reassurance in their maternal, rounded form. Would these dark hills speak of the darkly comforting God ever with him?

Then the drop down into Jedburgh, refreshment in the middle of such bleak country, refreshment between the Cambridge years and the Birmingham years. Faces from the past to bring memories flooding back, unforgotten acts of ministry greatly treasured; beloved faces whose absence would make the heart ache; predominantly new faces indicating how things have moved on these thirty years.

Jedburgh church had produced a booklet to mark its hundred-and-fiftieth, featuring its past rectors. The language about John Habgood is curiously veiled. It records how delighted the people were to have such a distinguished person in their midst; how they frequently released him for the wider Church's ministry; how he broadened Jedburgh's outlook with monthly meetings to discuss various meaty issues in Church and Society; how he worked for ecumenical understanding; how he introduced an international dimension by urging the parish to sponsor a Ghanaian student at Edinburgh Theological College.

But it also records how the Church School was closed down a year into his time there; how a national decline in church membership also made itself felt at Jedburgh; how it did not surprise the church when John Habgood decided to return to academic work.

The attempt at objective analysis somehow left a sour taste, that considerable success and considerable disappointment both featured in his ministry there. Yet why should the taste be sour? In recommending the ordained ministry, John Habgood seems all too well aware of the depths as well as the heights, that success can prove a false goal and is seldom final, that even failure as enormous as Calvary is not finally ratal. He enthuses about the ministry from a deep knowledge which I can only guess was forged at Jedburgh.

A postscript to end my speculation. The Archbishop has a very useful book which I often borrow, unexcitingly called *The Diocesan Service Book*. It is a fount of prayers for consecrations, dedications, and countless other things with which a bishop has to do. In the frontpiece is John Habgood's signature together with what I presume was the date of purchase: 1965. The book is all but useless to anyone who is not a bishop: I wonder if a door briefly opened in Jedburgh that year and let the future in?

18 OCTOBER

If anyone should think that residents of York will have been untouched by the Sheffield super-tram's wiles, they would be badly mistaken. Sheffield is one of the dioceses in the Northern Province, so is regularly visited by the Archbishop. Its cathedral suffers from being in the very centre of a city besieged by the super-tram, or rather the roadworks its creation has necessitated. Of all the places in all the Province which we visit, Sheffield Cathedral has the most difficult travelling time to gauge, primarily because the roadworks foul up our calculations. We will find ourselves on the wrong hill (Sheffield, like Rome, seems to perch on seven) or on the wrong side of the railway line (the Styx is easier to cross than that track) or going the wrong way through a one-way system with changed priorities.

The worst ever diversion occurred on this very night in 1992, but with some (surprisingly) superb navigation from me, we arrived at the Cathedral in the nick of time. Which was just as well, since the service was being televised. British Coal had just announced the mass closure of most of its mines and the Media had been tipped off that John Habgood would pass some comment in this Coal City. We robed in record time, assembled the telescopic primatial cross and tagged on to the back of the procession. Fortunately we are always at the very end, which tonight was a distinct advantage.

But as I was leading the Archbishop, cross in hand, it dawned upon me that we had not a clue where we were sitting. 'Do you know where we're going?' I muttered back to my boss.

'No,' he said, as calm as ever. 'Ask the churchwarden in front of you.' So I did. One of the wardens turned around, keeping up with the procession by walking backwards and said with great dignity, in his very best Sheffield dialect, 'Your Grace, you're sitting at the 'igh Halter.'

The Archbishop raised an amused eyebrow. 'Then that's where we'll go,' he said, his lips twitching towards a smile despite his iron self-control.

The service was to mark the anniversary of St Luke's Hospice in the city, so to combine this worthy event with coalmines posed quite a dilemma. But the Archbishop took it all in his masterly stride, beginning with the words, 'There is a good way to die and there is a bad way to die . . .' All else followed. The insensitive handling of the coalmines' closure was inevitably likened to insensitive handling of death, which the Hospice movement had done so much to correct.

I have never witnessed such an accolade for the Archbishop as was at the reception that followed that service. Ladies with even the deepest shade of blue hair applauded what he had said. The Conservative MP, certainly no Wet, felt the Archbishop was absolutely right and the closure of the mines was a crying shame.

Yet closed they were, despite this unanimous opposition. What went wrong?

'You're always here, these days,' perky Sister Stella Mary said to me as we bumped into each other yet again in the Minster. She is one of the nuns who surround the place with their prayers and give it a warm, human face. It is worth returning to the Minster just for her.

We had also come for the annual Children's Society service, a national event involving all walks of life connected with the Society. There was a family feel. As we waited outside the Zouche chapel to process in, the Archbishop pointed to the back of the Bishop of Worcester's mitre, 'Look, he's got a rear light!' The good Bishop (there because he was chairman of the Children's Society) had got a reflective silver cross on the back of his mitre as well as the front, hence the quip.

Representing the Church in Wales' connection with children was the Bishop of Bangor; a high point in the whole proceedings was his reading a collect in Welsh. His mitre did not have a rear light. Clearly Welsh bishops are more adept at avoiding processional shunts; or perhaps there are not enough of them around to crash.

Something akin to the international date-line had been cunningly installed in the Minster. I noticed that as we walked down the long central aisle accompanied by the processional hymn, one instant I was singing verse two, then next verse four, with no verse three in between. At the end, on the walk back down, I had to sing verse two of the recessional twice. The reason for this disorientating effect was that the congregation at the back were dragging the hymns, oblivious to the organ and choir keeping time at the east end. It all gave me the spiritual equivalent of jet lag.

The major work of the Society had moved away from funding institutions and homes to funding local projects which enabled disadvantaged children. PACT, such a local project in York, gave an arresting presentation. PACT provided carers for disabled children to give their parents and families much needed time out, as one placard proclaimed. The carers were clearly devoted to and adored by their charges. Their charges seemed thrilled to join in the presentation and service; one lad was tickled to bits at the end when the Archbishop allowed him to wear his mitre for a photo opportunity. The mitre suited him; Crown Appointments' Commission please note.

The story of Jairus' daughter which preceded the Archbishop's sermon clearly moved him. The tale of a dead girl raised to life seemed to the Archbishop to be the essence of what the Children's Society was about. Whilst its origins lay in tending children orphaned by the death of parents, these days it addressed children who were the victims of other deaths. These included emotional death, moral death, the death that comes through being undervalued, demeaned . . . All members of the Society aimed to raise these children from whatever death assailed them by love; a love which had to be immensely patient, since there were no quick fix results.

The Archbishop noted that the dead little girl in the gospel story was surrounded by a crowd of well-intentioned adults who made a lot of fuss but achieved precisely nothing. Talk and frantic activity were not enough.

First came an admission that behind emotionally crippled children were emotionally crippled adults, that society was a wounded place with wounds being passed from generation to generation. At the end of the day, these wounds could only begin to be healed by a love exemplified by Jesus, who took all society's aggression and hurt unto himself on the cross, absorbing the hate, triumphing in the midst of the direst tragedy. Those weighed down by death in whatever form it came needed to hear his voice in the voice of those around them, 'Little girl, I say to you, arise.'

The new Dean (how long will he bear the title 'new'?) welcomed us, still cheerful despite his continuing bronchitis. 'If you think this is damp, you wait till November,' were my only words of comfort. Perhaps not the voice one wants to hear when weighed down by a deadly Vale of York chill.

1 NOVEMBER

'I will look unto the hills from whence cometh my help.' You did not have to look far with the distinctive mount rising like a giant behind the village, casting its long shadow upon it. Long ago, people must have worshipped the mount as a god; perhaps they still did; certainly countless modern pilgrims trod their way to the top.

The nearby peak standing over and above us well illustrated the Archbishop's sermon this All Saintstide as he spoke of the powers that surround us. He spoke of saintliness in the people who were near to us; saintliness in the people who enlarged us and loved us into being and faith; saintliness in the people we could see through, not because they were false, but because they let God shine through, just like the anaemic saints in stained-glass windows let the light shine through; saintliness in the people who did away with pretence and were big enough to be real and encourage us to own our reality.

The Archbishop's clarity contrasted with the rather confused way the service was ordered. Instead of sitting on the front row the candidates were scattered throughout the congregation, flecks-in-marble style. It was a nice expression of their integration; hopeless though, when the Archbishop tried to address them as a group and instill some cohesion. And all a bit of a muddle when they stepped out to be confirmed, since you genuinely did not know where the next candidate was going to pop up from.

The church had just been reordered, tastefully decorated, with an unusual arrangement of communion rail which dictated a complex one-way system. Unfortunately the maze foxed most communicants which meant that the Archbishop was penned in, with an empty rail before him, no one there to receive the bread of life he had to offer. I had the funniest feeling there was a parable lurking there somewhere.

The hall was packed for the reception afterwards with lively people, flushed with faith. It was clearly a pioneer church, the unusual arrangement of the service and reordering indicative of a priest and people on the frontiers, experimenting, pushing out the boundaries. And clearly such a dynamic was producing saints in their scores, saints who were bold enough not to miss singing 'For all the saints . . . ' this All Saints' Day. To go without such a lovely hymn is a mark of true saintliness I have yet to achieve.

3 NOVEMBER

Sometimes the Archbishop sheds twenty years, as he did a year ago. The expected delays on the A1 never materialized, so we approached Durham hopelessly early. 'Gordon, let's go to Bishop Auckland,' the Archbishop suggested.

So we detoured to his former home, parking near the gate and peeping in. The Archbishop was boylike in his enthusiasm, 'Look, there's the chapel, there's the Diocesan Office . . .' Although we only stayed a few minutes, since the Archbishop was keen not to intrude on his successor's privacy, we nevertheless got the flavour of the place. Our escape, however, was blocked by a refuse lorry; its driver was so flustered with having an Archbishop's limo draw up behind him, that he shot off, with wheely bin still attached to the back. Some poor soul would be binless for a while.

Over the years the Archbishop and his wife have passed a few comments about Auckland Castle. The vastness of the place after their Birmingham flat, forcing them to raid auction rooms for cheap furniture to fill the spaces. The miles and miles of corridors they had to walk down to tend sick children. The luxury of being able to walk out of the gate straight into Marks and Spencer's to buy sandwiches for lunch (and having the salary which could afford them).

The grounds were vast too, a veritable park. Twenty minutes after setting off from the Castle, with Gordon driving at a fair rate, the Archbishop spurted out, 'I think that's our back gate!' Most people take twenty seconds to walk to their back gate; we took twenty minutes to drive there!

His enthusiasm continued unabated when we got to University College for lunch, pointing out every nook and cranny which he had discovered over his ten years there. Significantly his favourite was a crypt-like chapel.

The lunch was very fine indeed; I had an excellent conversation with the Mayor who tried to prise out of me the name of Durham's new bishop so he could make a killing at the bookies. I kept my own counsel.

The Founders and Benefactors service was a crowded affair, but a very friendly one, with the Durham clergy going out of their way to be hospitable. The fullness of the cathedral paled into significance when the whole congregation gathered around Cuthbert's tomb for an important part of the memorial; it was positively scrum-like. Cuthbert certainly had company that day. And I was glad of my primatial cross to beat a way through the crowds.

The service over, we lingered in the airy Deanery for tea, with the Archbishop renewing contact with so many friends. There were lots of ghosts that day. Not only were we surrounded by all those Northern Saints, for whose generosity of spirit (or money) we gave thanks. A 46-year-old John Habgood also visited the place and possessed his own 66-year-old body. For a day I had a companion near my own age rather than a distant father in God.

12 NOVEMBER

The port of Hull was flattened in the last war. A people already insular and xenophobic have never really forgiven the Germans for doing that to them. So calling a big diocesan event '*Kirchentag*' (Churches Day in German) effectively excluded the Hull end of the Diocese from the outset. That was the first mistake.

The second mistake was not switching on the heating in the Minster on this chilly autumn day. The grand design for *Kirchentag* was that following stimulating lectures, buzz groups would meet all over the place to chat excitedly about various issues. It is difficult to feel excited sitting on cold stone with white clouds of your breath puffing out before you every time you speak.

The third mistake was out of our hands. One of the speakers cancelled at the last moment, so everything had to be rescheduled. Bishop Holloway from the frozen wastes of Edinburgh (hardly more frozen than the Minster that day) was to have been the sweeper-upper, dropping in on the groups, listening to them and producing a patchwork quilt of their deliberations in a final address. Now he had to be a main speaker and the lot of sweeping up fell to the Archbishop.

And so we tiptoed amongst the groups, desperately searching for pearls of wisdom. I admired the way the Archbishop did the job, but inevitably having an archbishop sidle up to your group had a somewhat intimidating effect on whoever was speaking at the time. The children's groups were less self-conscious, although precisely what they were doing other than having a lot of fun with old cereal packets, paints, and paste remained to be seen. Amazingly the Archbishop was unsplattered by paint and paste, resisted the temptation to prove his DIY skills with cornflake packets and managed a stirring finale, proving his enviable skill of being able to make bricks out of straw.

Notwithstanding the excellence of the speakers, the day was a flop. Probably because the Church's strength does not lie in big events such as this where enthusiasm has to be whipped up, but rather lies in the parishes. The heart of the Christian gospel is that God did not throw a big jamboree in heaven, call it a clever name, and issue invitations. He came down to where people were. That is the essence of Incarnation which the Archbishop humbly reflects as he trudges from parish to parish, big and small, well-attended and ill-attended, reaching out in the steps of history's supreme reacher-outer.

We were almost blown all the way to Hull. Certainly we were driving too fast to stop in that thriving metropolis and found ourselves at the dark side of the black hole, heading towards Spurn Point at the mouth of the Humber.

With a little time to spare we drove to the riverside village of Paul, although since the Humber is so wide at that point it almost feels like being at the seaside. Having slipped off his cassock, the Archbishop strolled on the front with that faraway look in his eye.

The scenery certainly was striking. To the west was the Humber Bridge, its full span visible because of the river's meander. The River Hull flowed into the Humber further downstream, with the city sprawling around it, seemingly small and safe at this distance. Saltend refinery belched out its fumes, imitated by its cousins on the river's south bank. A North Sea ferry glided past us, its passengers in for a very rough crossing indeed as it sailed east into a bleak horizon. The Archbishop stood there and contemplated it all, God's stranger on the shore. A bridge, a city, a spoiled creation, a boat, a boundless horizon: your spiritual poverty would have to be deep indeed for you to remain untouched by such images.

Then the Archbishop's eyes lost their misty look and he snapped, 'It's about time we got going.' So off we sped from Paul, with the Archbishop wriggling into his cassock in the back of the car.

As we drove along, the wind deteriorated to storm, with rain falling like stair rods. I was alarmed that the deeper we got into South Holderness, field after field was submerged, almost as if the whole peninsula was being deliberately flooded.

We reached our destination only to discover that our way was impeded down the church path by the torrent which bisected it. Much of South Holderness is barely at sea level, but is kept dry by an ingenious system of drains. On that particular morning a fallen tree had blocked one of them, so that when the tide came in the water found whatever channels it could, which unfortunately took a virtual river through the graveyard.

Gordon kindly reversed the limo through the torrent and we scrambled out onto the church steps, our feet only slightly damp. An enterprising farmer used his Landrover to shuttle people across so that at least we had a congregation.

All this excitement meant that things were not as well prepared in the church as they might have been. Ironically, we had a tremendous problem finding any water for the cruet for the Eucharist. But eventually we got under way.

The New Testament Lesson was poignant indeed, containing Hebrews' comment on the Exodus: 'By faith the people crossed the Red Sea as if on dry land.' Having crossed our own sea that morning, I was surprised the Archbishop was able to resist preaching on the text.

The service ended, we paddled to the village hall for an Act of Remembrance, timed to the second by Big Ben's chimes on a car radio. I glanced at the War Memorial; even a village as tiny as this had sacrificed dozens of her sons. The bugler played the last call, after which we should have stood in silence for two minutes. The gale was so fierce, however, that it blew us all into the hall after two seconds. After a long welcome by the local Methodist preacher, we got to the real business of the day and gratefully swigged a cup of hot strong tea, a sort of nonconformist communion.

Having sung 'Eternal Father, strong to save, whose arm doth bind the restless wave,' we decided that the wave was still far too restless for our liking, so we scuttled home. South Holderness survived the storm; this time.

A Press Conference: the Archbishop is an old hand on such Press occasions, unruffled even by Jeremy Paxman. But despite their frequency, one conference will always remain fixed in my memory . . .

The four reporters fidgeted and shuffled their bottoms as they sat before the Archbishop, the low autumn sun streaming through the windows and dazzling them. One was clearly bored and gazed around the room waiting for things to start; another began to pick his nose.

I might add at this point that the reporters were all aged eleven, two boys and two girls. The Archbishop had graciously agreed to give them an interview for their school magazine, an act made even more gracious by his honouring the commitment despite being laid low by a severe dose of flu. So there they were, with legs dangling over the settee, under the eagle eye of their clearly anxious headmaster.

The questions had been drawn up by them, but then vetted beforehand. For instance the poser, 'Are you an archbishop all the time or do you have a proper job?' had been firmly ruled out. But there was still some provocative stuff. 'How do you justify the church's wealth and extravagance?' was greeted with a straight bat.

'Only the best is good enough for God; the best material for robes, the best buildings for churches. We have to give God our very best,' the Archbishop explained.

'Although he can cope rather well with dirty stables and bloody crosses,' I silently added.

One of the girl cub reporters, obviously destined for a dazzling career in putting people on the spot, asked, 'When I'm grown up, will you ordain me?' This was before the General Synod's vote to approve the ordination of women to the priesthood, so was a delicate issue to say the least (although the

Archbishop's role in keeping the two sides together is still a delicate one now).

But again the diplomatic expertise of the Archbishop shone through, 'I rather think your ambition at this time in your life should be to grow up and be a good Christian. Let that come first. But tell me, do you really want to be ordained?'

The girl wavered. 'I'm not sure,' she replied, and the subject was safely passed over.

The session was extremely impressive, with a wide range of subject material, handled well by reporters and Archbishop alike. Most impressive was the children's seemingly innate understanding of the Archbishop's pauses. He often stops in mid-sentence to think through an answer. Adults often make the mistake of leaping in and answering for him, or moving on to the next subject. The children showed themselves with much more skill than that: they patiently gave spacc and waited so that the Archbishop was able to frame his answer perfectly. As he commented at the end, 'This is the best and kindest interview with the Press I've ever had.'

It was a typical Vale of York fog, a pea-souper, damp and chill, weighing down the soul. Slowly we wound our way, with Gordon peering through the windscreen, familiar landmarks totally obliterated, the swirling mist conferring an anonymity on well-known places, which popped up with alarming suddenness. Crossing the River Derwent at Stamford Bridge was an inevitable point of identification. At least geographically we knew where we were, but the fog, aided by just a little imagination, transported you to a different age: shouts of fear from the routed Vikings, shouts of triumph from Harold and his men, blissfully unaware of the deadly defeat that lay ahead of them in a less hospitable south.

We left Stamford Bridge and our voices behind and began to crawl up Garrowby Hill to the top of the Wolds. Just before the summit, Lord Halifax's crucifix loomed through the fog. Perhaps I ought to explain that this was not the means by which a former Lord Halifax had been cruelly executed, but was rather a large crucifix, erected by him to the glory of God and, quaintly, to the memory of King George VI. Curiously, as we reached this point the fog cleared to reveal a blazing sun and clear blue sky, with the blanket of cloud left behind.

This offered an irresistible illustration for the Archbishop's sermon—climbing out of the fog, towards Jesus with the light beyond. An obvious theme, but none the less brilliant, perhaps more appreciated by those who had made the journey from darkness to light than by the good people of Flamborough, who had enjoyed uninterrupted sunshine all morning.

Even so, the Archbishop had a good rapport with the congregation, (a massive one with a massive choir for so small a village) who seemed well attuned to his natural holiness. In the middle of his sermon he embarked on a career of hitherto unsuspected radical New Testament scholarship by positing the end of Mark's Gospel in the middle of Jesus' trial, claiming the Gospel concluded with chapter fourteen.

Realizing that this, amongst other things, would have robbed Lord Halifax of his aforesaid memorial he soon lost his nerve (or realized his mistake) and reinstated the missing two chapters with an apologetic grin, 'Did I say fourteen? Of course, I meant sixteen!' The congregation nodded, trying to look like a symposium of New Testament experts rather than give away the fact that they had never even noticed he had said anything at all unusual.

By our return to Garrowby the fog had completely cleared, so that Jesus on his cross now looked down on the Vale of York in all its dazzling glory, framed by the Dales beyond. Before us was a patchwork quilt of field upon field; towering York Minster, its white limestone caught in the sun's rays; the cooling towers of Drax, Eggborough, and Ferrybridge—the trinity of power stations with their tell-tale trail of steam bound for Scandinavia with our love; the Humber, a thin silver pencil perched on the horizon.

The Lord Halifax who had installed the cross was, as Viceroy of India, Foreign Secretary and then Ambassador to America, a much travelled man. Yet he described his home at Garrowby as having the best view in all the world. That morning we knew how right he was.

28 NOVEMBER

General Synod in London: not a phrase to set the pulse racing, I fear. It is a much maligned body, since more often than not the subjects on its agenda are those an attentive church should be addressing, with many humorous and informed speeches generally extending one's knowledge of whatever topic is under discussion.

Whether in London or York, Raymond Barker (the Archbishop's Lay Assistant) and I sit behind the Archbishop, ostensibly to brief him. Since the Archbishop is near omniscient and brooks no briefing, we have to do our best to look wise and act as if we are needed. The Archbishop of Canterbury, who sits alongside our Archbishop, kindly asks our opinion or borrows some document from us from time to time to make us feel wanted.

That is not to say John Habgood does not consult. Only last Synod he gave me a message to take to the Secretary General's secretary (a specialist in tautology), along the lines of 'Let's have lunch ten minutes earlier.' I walked on to the platform and whispered into the Secretary General's secretary's ear with the importance of one mouthing urgent issues of state. He whispered to his boss who whispered back to him who whispered back to me. I walked off with due solemnity and in turn whispered to my boss 'OK'. I hope the Synod were duly impressed.

I prefer Synod at York University primarily because I can cycle to it. Over the Ouse at the Bishopthorpe railway bridge (mercifully the line is no longer used, so I do not encounter the Flying Scotsman) and then past the Naburn sewage works and former mental hospital. A fitting preparation, some might think, for the meeting which lies ahead.

Worship at York is definitely not Synod at its best, since it tries to please too many people by catering to every colour of the

Anglican spectrum. The worship 'booklet' for the weekend almost runs to several volumes, too wordy for a God (and Archbishop) whose ultimate refuge is silence. Even so, it comes as an immense shock to you as you walk through the doors of the University Church at 7.00 a.m. to see the place full of all the C of E's famous names, all squashed together.

On Sunday the Synod moves to the Minster for much improved worship, primarily because the Minster has an expertise which even with a Mozart Mass allows for a welcoming lightness of touch. Archbishops' chaplains walk in side by side, primatial crosses vying for the highest place, with their respective archbishops walking behind in a similar duet. One will preach, the other will celebrate, presenting an irresistible opportunity to compare the two men.

George Carey is big enough to defer to John Habgood. Perhaps not surprisingly considering the latter's stature; the fact that, in another incarnation as Bishop of Durham, John Habgood inducted George Carey as vicar of St Nicholas, the Church in the Market Place (to coin a phrase), also sets a stamp of deference. Even so, lesser men would try to score points, pull rank. George Carey is more immense than that.

There is also an immense warmth. George Carey is alert, notices people, in so doing conveying a sense that they are valued. For instance, I often wear a stole which I had specially designed for my ordination. The motif on it is intricate, combining my college crest with the doctrine of fall and redemption, quite an achievement in a few inches of brocade. My Archbishop has never noticed it, or if he has, has said nothing. Within minutes of our first meeting at York Minster, the Archbishop of Canterbury asked, interestedly, 'And what does all this symbolize?'

He is good with the family too, always a word and a hug for the little girls, a word for Rachel, whom he recognized as a teacher from the very start. 'How did you know what my job was?' she asked, amused.

'From the way you were showing your daughters how to follow the service,' he remarked. Now there is attentiveness for you, mirroring the One who saw Nathaniel under a fig tree and knew him in an instant.

The ABY and the ABC (as they are abbreviated in countless minutes). A good team; a good balanced ticket, complementing each other, both with qualities and skills which are better distinct rather than duplicated.

4 DECEMBER

We were too late for the Illuminations and too early for Christmas, but at least the drive to Blackpool was enjoyable. We climbed out of an overcast Leeds early on Sunday morning, winding up the M62, the grass on the peaks crisp white with frost, standing to attention as we drove by. At the watershed the weather changed dramatically and we dropped into a sunny Lancashire, although the clear blue sky was unable to tempt a grey Irish sea to change colour.

Arriving in Blackpool ahead of schedule, we decided our before-dawn start warranted a trip to the Front, if we could find it. After a couple of abortive attempts necessitating a seven-point turn in narrow terraced streets surprised by an Archbishop's limo, we had a brisk drive along a front whose high wall nicely prevented us from seeing the sea. Gordon stopped in a lorry park with high security fencing (not one of Blackpool's beauty spots) and by the time the Archbishop had slipped off his cassock we barely had seconds to peep over the fence and glimpse the Golden Mile before rushing back to be in church on time.

The Archbishop has been a bit funny about where he is seen with his cassock on ever since that aside on *Have I Got News For You*. Angus Deayton summarized the House of Bishops' report, *Issues in Human Sexuality*, as condemning priests in an active gay relationship. 'The report was presented at a news conference by three men wearing purple dresses with big gold necklaces dangling down their chests,' he smugly remarked; with the result that I have noticed a certain touchiness whenever we have appeared cassocked in public.

To be honest, I'm past caring and will sport my cassock anywhere; what was good enough for a Cossack is good enough for me. But I also feel that one is more likely to draw attention to oneself wriggling out of a cassock in the back of a car parked in a lorry park, with curious truckers looking on, than one ever would by not bothering to take the thing off in the first place.

Our first official engagement in Blackpool was a church whose roof was deliberately ribbed to look like an upturned hull. By definition all naves are supposed to have some resemblance to a boat, but this one was so convincing a replica that as a member of the congregation you began to feel as if you were an extra in the film *The Poseidon Adventure*.

The church was not only nautical, but ultra high, with genuflections at every colon. They were kind enough to supply the Archbishop with his own local chaplain, which made me, who had travelled over the Pennines for the express purpose, feel somewhat redundant. The home chaplain overfussed the Archbishop, presenting him his mitre at every turn, like an anxious assistant in a millinery department desperate to get madam to try on all the hats in their range. After a while I was redundant no longer, since I found myself a role whispering in his ear to lay off, or words to that effect.

A unique ritual at the Offertory featured one of the servers juggling with a cruet of red wine, which promptly disgorged its contents over his alb. Perhaps the change in liturgical colour from white to red marked an important movement in the liturgy at that point.

The Mass was followed by a cuppa in a vast church hall, smelling, as so many do, of that subtle blend of mouse droppings and Harpic. An old lady, wrapped around in an off-brown carpet of a coat which must have been the very height of fashion in the spring 1922 collection, was kind enough to lecture me on the perils of women priests. I was indebted to her and deeply moved that the action of the Mass, clearly of such moment to them all, had failed to impinge on such sheer, unadulterated prejudice. It is sobering to realize that there are some things that even Christ's healing touch cannot change.

Our lunch was at a public school craftily sited on a peninsula, buffeted by wind from every compass point and chilled by a frozen sea. Even if the three Rs passed the pupils by, they would certainly have a bracing education. A delicious buffet lunch, with tedium relieved by an ever humorous Bishop of Lancaster, was followed by a very formal service indeed.

The high point was a choir consisting of uniformed *nursery* children who sang 'One more step along the road we go' impeccably. The Archbishop watched with rapt attention, not for a moment giving away the fact that he had been on the road since six. Whilst equally alert, I was not so rapt: the performance was too perfect. I prefer nursery school children's singing to be more off-key, their hats (if they *have* to wear them) to be more askew, their clothes more crumpled. In short I prefer under-fives to look as if they have got a few more steps to take rather than looking as if they have done it all. Oh dear, reactionary old me! Prejudice was obviously contagious on the West Coast.

After a snatched tea we got on the road. We might have missed the Blackpool Illuminations but we had our own on the M62 with a lighted ramp seemingly going up into heaven. The Lancashire roadlamps on the incline were on, the Yorkshire ones were off, hence the effect. With just a little imagination I cast myself as Elisha, Gordon as the fiery horseman of Israel, the limo as a chariot and the Archbishop as Elijah, all ascending into a heaven where even purple cassocks can be worn without embarrassment.

'Have you got anything on John the Baptist?' the Archbishop asked, out of the blue, one day. He was preparing a sermon for an Advent visit to a theological college.

I was flattered; at long last he had acknowledged my interest in the New Testament. Not only did I know that John was the forerunner of Jesus (a sort of primatial chaplain *par excellence*); I also had a few books on him. My favourite, by John Robinson, I passed on to the Archbishop.

'I can't be doing with all this radical stuff,' was his response. In that case we should never have ventured out of Bishopthorpe Palace's door, since the treat our theological college was to put on made John Robinson's radicalism seem about as controversial as the Queen's Christmas Day speech.

After a few hours' drive on a drizzly December day, when we eventually arrived in the city suburbs we were caught up in a Sunday street market. Several people rapped on the car window, trying to sell us bargain watches and novelty balloons as we crawled through the mayhem. I resisted the temptation and kept my door locked.

To say the least we were somewhat wearied by the time we reached the theological college, a little early for their midday Communion (the term Eucharist was suspiciously high for them.) Initially we had the distinct feeling we were intruding on the place's privacy. Having found the Common Room, we were largely ignored by students keen to get on with such urgent business as reading the Sunday papers, drinking coffee, and playing snooker. Eventually a jeans-clad youth of indeterminate sex came over to us, chewing gum. 'Are you the Bishop of York?' he casually asked.

'*Arch*bishop,' the Archbishop corrected him with a chill to his voice that the North Pole would have rejected for being too cold.

I felt the temptation to add, 'Take me to your leader,' but my mischievousness was thwarted by the principal bustling in, his Harris tweed jacket flapping.

'John, how good of you to come,' he boomed, in his best patronizing voice, betraying his expertise in pastoral studies and bereavement care. 'I trust you've been made welcome. I see you've already met Jim, the guestmaster.'

Jim the guestmaster, still chewing his gum, seemed to me to have been just a teeny weeny bit miscast in the role. Or perhaps we had caught him on a bad day. Still, it was good to have his gender clarified.

The principal bustled us to his study, which could easily have doubled up as a library. All the wall space was used for shelves, brimful with books. At various points on the floor stood a pillar of books, all leaning precariously like mini-towers of Pisa; I wondered how much of his time he spent finely balancing them all. Having cleared armfuls of books off the chairs he invited us to sit down.

As he chatted about the college he offered us sherry, which we declined, much to his puzzlement. 'Are you sure? I always have one before Communion.' The Archbishop's left eyebrow rose several millimetres, his fingers drumming on a pillar of books by his left arm, clear danger signals to say the least. As he poured himself a sherry, the principal was oblivious. With hindsight we should have joined him.

The clock struck twelve. 'Oh goodness! Time for prayers,' the principal blurted out, in much the same way that a mum would say 'Time for bed!' to her little chicks.

'It's all informal here, John, no need to robe. We'll just go into chapel as we are; feel free to sit where you want.' And so at the principal's bidding, in we went. Encouragingly the place was full. Gum-chewing Jim, the guestmaster, was there, squatting in a yoga position. Several were sitting cross-legged on the floor, like primary school children, awaiting assembly. Some sat on cushioned chairs, looking guilty for being such squares. The celebrant was easily identifiable: he was the one sitting behind the altar. Unfortunately the altar was high, his chair was low, with the result that we could only see his disembodied head; his chin perched, as it were, on the altar edge. There was a large earring hanging from one ear.

'Roight!' he said, in pure cockney, 'We're all 'ere, so we mite as well start. Cor, strike me, I nearly forgot, it's good to have John from York with us who'll give us a word or two later on. First, tho', let me tell you wat we're goin to do. We'll all be back 'ome on Christmas Day, so we thought we'd celebrate it early in college. As we all know, Christmas is about a birth. We thought we'd begin today by having Debbie, who used to be a midwife, to tell us all about obst, obstat, obstit, er, birth.'

A wide-hipped Debbie sauntered out to the front and launched into her spiel. Whilst birth is undoubtedly a natural process, by the time she had concluded I was convinced that it was distinctly lacking in delicacy. After a long car journey, I was not feeling too well anyway; her all too vivid description of the pain and gore that the Virgin Mary and other women endured brought the bile into my mouth.

I started taking deep breaths just like one of her patients, but mercifully without the contractions. However, I was soon joined by others. 'Come on,' implored Debbie. 'I want to hear you all pant, the Pant of Life!' The whole body of students started breathing heavily. I stopped the deep breaths. The Archbishop never started, although he clearly needed them: he was looking in a bad way.

Having exhausted her repertoire of tales to make the flesh creep, Debbie gave back the reins to the celebrant, who announced the first hymn—if it could be called a hymn. It went something like, 'Did you sleep in the straw, Jesus child; did it tickle your nose, Jesus child?' The students swayed to the refrain, 'Jesus, Jesus, Jesus child'. John of York did not sway.

The ditty subsided, and then the poem, *The Oxen* by Thomas Hardy (my favourite) was read. It was by a long chalk the most numinous thing so far. This was followed by silence, although students were encouraged to revoice the Pant of Life, if they felt so inclined. There were more pants in that chapel than in a Marks and Spencer's warehouse.

Once everyone had run out of breath, the gospel was read, no gimmicks, Luke 2.1–7. It was followed by the Archbishop's very erudite sermon on John the Baptist, a somewhat surprising intrusion into this jolly Christmas scene. He had not even been mentioned hitherto, nor was mentioned afterto.

Once the sermon was over, the rest of the service went on fast-forward. I recall little detail. The offertory hymn was a Showaddywaddy hit from the 1970s, 'Will you be lonely this Christmas, without someone to hold?' Not one of the Archbishop's favourites, I fear. But he endured it all, until the end provided the last straw (presumably no longer tickling Jesus' nose). An impromptu choir struck up 'Jingle Bells', complete with sleigh bells. The Archbishop reddened in fury, strode out and slammed the door behind him.

Then I awoke: a child had slammed a door downstairs and disturbed my nightmare. I was in no theological college, but tucked up in bed at home. As I rubbed my eyes, reality flooded in, a reality so different from my dream. All the theological colleges we had visited, all I had visited as Director of Ordinands, paraded in my imagination, institutions so worthy. I saw lines of students, not jeans-clad nonentities, but rather people alive to God, brimming with faith, primed for ministry. I pictured the staff, not inept, not parodies, but immensely noble men and women, sensitive and shrewd, all too aware of the privilege and charge the Church had laid upon them to furnish the ministry of the future. I pictured the worship, well-balanced, thoughtful, prayerful.

And I thought of the Archbishop, who never, ever, got angry or slammed doors. Even so, I made a mental note to leave 'Jingle Bells' off the chapel music list. Dreams can have a very nasty habit of fulfilling themselves; at least if the Bible is anything to go by.

WINTER

21 DECEMBER

Christmas is coming and Gordon the chauffeur is dispatched to York Railway Station to pick up the royal venison, graciously granted to the Archbishop by the Royal Household. I fully expected him to return with a deer draped across his shoulders, so was immensely disappointed to find him sheepishly walking up the drive sporting only two plastic carrier bags.

The contents of one is stewed up and served for the staff Christmas party. 'Mm, how delicious!' everyone enthuses. No one is brave enough to liken it to braising steak still needing a couple of hours' good boil.

Tough venison not withstanding, the party is superb. The table is decked beautifully with crackers and streamers galore, red serviettes folded like mitres (inevitably), steaming vegetables and an inexhaustible supply of Mrs Habgood's Yorkshire pudding. Lunch is served on the some-twenty-foot-long oak Tudor table, allegedly made with the timber from just one tree. Those on the west side have their backs roasted by the log fire, crackling in the grate. Those on the east side have their backs frozen by the chill draft from the windows, only feet below which the icy swollen Ouse has burst its banks. Despite the severe temperature gradient, everyone is jolly, everyone has a party hat perched on them, with the Archbishop, well used to wearing silly hats, looking the least self-conscious.

After lunch comes the archiepiscopal slide show, with guests trying so desperately hard not to slumber after being so well wined and dined. The Archbishop's best display was undoubtedly his slides of South Africa, impeccably careful studies of giraffes juxtaposed with native huts and veldt that stretched for miles. Less good was the year when we had a video of a hospital in South Africa, where Zulus, eager to display their grasp of AIDS prevention danced a hokey-cokey chanting 'Say no to sex!' I sat there wondering how I was going to explain *that* to my children afterwards. The worst year was when the Archbishop showed his snaps of a recent visit to Auschwitz, his commentary giving a chillingly scientific account of the capacity and use of the ovens. One began to feel distinctly queezy.

Ghosts and memories abound since I have treasured parties at Bishopthorpe for over thirty years. When I was a boy, Donald Coggan, a former archbishop, used to host Christmas parties for clergy children and organized edifying games.

One such game which considerably confused me was 'biblical partners', with the simple rule that you were allotted a biblical name and had to find your biblical counterpart. I was given the name David, already my Christian name, hence the confusion. I recall Donald Coggan saying in his crisp tone which brooked no discussion, 'You're David' and my replying, 'Yes, that's right,' only to be followed by his exasperated insistence, 'No, you-are-David.' And so it went on, until finally the penny dropped; I went hunting and found my Goliath lurking beneath the portrait of William Temple.

Later biblical study, of which I was then blissfully oblivious, revealed a fairly long list of candidates for the post of David's partner, although I am not sure what reception Abishag, Abigail, and Bathsheba would have received in an austere 1960s Bishopthorpe. Even so, my later list was not as long as one senior bishop reckoned, when I related the episode to him. 'Yes, of course,' he quipped. 'David's partner could have been Delilah.' Although David was a notorious sexual athlete, even he drew the line at necrophilia.

Time has gone on and the children's parties are no more, thank God. I remember nervous chaplains asking us repeatedly whether we needed the lavatory. Obviously there had been a serious mishap at a previous party and chaplains ever after had been ordered to guard the carpets, or else. I also recall parents driven to distraction by fears that their offspring, in an unguarded moment, might let slip some expletive ('Damn' was enough to defrock you in those days) or relay some conversation conducted in some shady corner of a vicarage never meant for the ears of the Senior Staff.

24 DECEMBER

Dark; Christmas Eve: York Minster, absolutely packed from door to door, transept to transept, Choir to Nave, with people, all hoping it might be so. Nine Lessons, even more carols, in one of Europe's largest cathedrals, all celebrating that the smallest stable was the birthplace of the son of God twenty centuries ago. The atmosphere was pregnant and electric, hardened clergy robing in vestries, who had done the show countless times before, as excited as the most innocent child.

The cast was predictable: the choir, men and boys; the canons, major and minor; the Dean; the Archbishop. In service layout I am always described as the Cross of York; very cross of York might be a better description, since I dislike having anonymity thrust upon me.

The star of the show as far as I am concerned is the Apparitor, Richard Bundy, the Head Verger. A highly honourable man of great substance, he always has the service sussed out and tips me off about where to stand and walk, advice which repeatedly proves invaluable. Since in order of procession he leads me, should I forget his careful instructions simply 'follow that verger!' is the order of the day. However important the occasion, however famous the celebrities, Richard remains the same, calm, unruffled, constant. Every visit to the Minster drives me to thank God for his guidance.

And guidance is what I certainly need at the Carol Service, with a veritable walkabout through the crowds. The service proper starts with a trembling treble's solo of 'Once in Royal David's City', then in we walk, from the West Door, through the Nave into the Choir for a few short lessons to get your breath back, then back to the Tower crossing for a further breather before a return to the Choir and High Altar. One of these years I will stick a pedometer to my cross and clock up the miles; one certainty is that I will awake to celebrate the Saviour's birth with aching arms and legs: how can I ever forget him?

The choir's repertoire varies each year, the singing always crystal clear. Considering the fact that women comprise fifty per cent of the human race, and that one woman's 'Let it be' started off the whole show, I grieve that women do not play a more major part on this occasion. Sometimes there is a token woman reading a lesson, sometimes none at all. And they say apartheid is dead.

The final lesson, the Prologue of John's Gospel, is read by the Archbishop, with voice measured, reverent, full of awe: 'And the Word became flesh and dwelt amongst us, full of grace and truth.' As the Archbishop speaks, he speaks for every man, woman, and child in that five-thousand-strong congregation, a hungry multitude who listen enthralled as they are fed with the Bread of Life. The Archbishop is only there because that Word was made that Flesh; the rest of us are only there because that Word was made that Flesh; the Minster only exists (lest she forget it) because that Word was made that Flesh. In the triune name of that Word the Archbishop blesses the congregation and we depart into the night: Christmas has truly begun.

8 JANUARY

The Ouse had been rising all night as the thaw took hold upstream in the Dales. First to flood is the ings (low meadowland) to the east of the meander. Next the river rises 13 ft above its normal level and starts to seep over the wall into the Palace terraces. The rose garden is the first victim, the pruned trees disappearing under the rising water. Then the sundial is submerged. Finally the front lawn is invaded and the trickle into the cellar begins. The wood store has been moved to drier climes and we leave Bishopthorpe in the hope that the flood has reached its peak. Otherwise we will be rowing back up the drive.

Our destination: another visit to a mercifully dry Sheffield, not to the Cathedral this time but to St Mark's, Broomhall, for a service attended by scientists who are Christians (though not Christian Scientists). The kind vicar had laid out a china tea service in the vestry and proffered us a cuppa; since, like Tony Benn, I'm a definite tea addict, I wished more clergy would follow his gracious example for our visits.

I am very fond of St Mark's, the church in which Rachel and I were married several years before, and had briefed the Archbishop carefully. The church was firebombed in the war; the vicar's absence with the only set of keys had hindered the fire brigade's entry, so the building was gutted. But by the 1960s a new church had arisen out of the ashes, designed by the renowned George Pace. There were many original and daring touches which earned the new building the accolade of being described as England's forty-third cathedral. The Archbishop was well aware of all this as I proudly showed him round. 'Hmm. A bit concrete-blockish!' was the only comment he could muster.

10 JANUARY

Preparations were under way for my daughter Hannah's fourth birthday party. Chocolate dainties had been made in their scores, every flavour of crisp under the sun had been purchased, the cake had been designed and now awaited Henry Moore to sculpt it. We even hit on a present, not easy when you have an elder sister who has already got everything that is going. All that remained was to send out the invitations; 'Hannah, who shall we ask, who do you really want?' we implored.

Typically Hannah took time to decide, but then was adamant. 'The Archbishop and Little Luke,' she said, firmly. Little Luke, I am afraid, was elusive, since we did not know his surname. There was an amazingly long list of Lukes, little or otherwise, in my daughter's acquaintance. One could hardly ring up the parents of each and ask about their son's size before issuing a party invitation.

Having thus failed with Little Luke, the Archbishop was at least identifiable, but who would dare ask a Primate to interrupt his busy day to attend a little girl's birthday party? Hannah's birthday dawned and I still had not broached the subject. She pleaded with her big birthday hazel eyes, 'Daddy, you haven't asked the Archbishop yet, have you? Please let him come.'

Spurred on by her eloquent appeal, and encouraged by Mary, the Archbishop's Private Secretary, I plucked up the courage. I was genuinely surprised by his willingness. 'Just let me sign the day's letters, then I'll come along,' was his response. He sounded quite keen; at least more keen than I ever am to endure a child's birthday party.

At five o'clock the party shrieks of six little girls and two beleaguered boys were interrupted by a rap on the kitchen door. In came the Archbishop and everyone, mums as well as tinies, gaped open-mouthed in amazement. I guess as party turns go, my guest had trumped them all. Simply to have come would have been enough; but the Archbishop also brought entertainment. 'Do you know what I've got in my pocket?' he asked the enthralled children. Not being privy to the contents of Primate's pockets, they answered him not a word.

'Well, it's a snake's egg,' he explained, in the sort of voice that suggested that surely it was obvious that every Archbishop always carried one about his person. He showed them something like a tiny bean. 'Would you like to hatch it out?' They nodded, although clinging to each other, wary of what might happen next. Having an Archbishop interrupt your party brandishing snake's eggs was enough to boggle the mind of even the most imaginative four-year-old. Several rubbed their eyes to check they were not dreaming.

With great care the Archbishop placed the 'egg' on a saucer on our newly linoed floor. He then struck a match and teased the egg with it. Nothing happened, but then after a long pause the whole thing came to life, sizzling and erupting, spewing a long hot snake-like mass straight onto my pristine lino. 'There you are, children. I told you it was a snake's egg,' said the Archbishop with the pride of a scientist proved right. Whilst I did not want to spoil the boss's moment of glory, I felt the snake looked more like something the border terriers had done, affectionately known in the Palace grounds as 'bombs' (which would make for a confusing time if we ever had a terrorist raid).

After a quick word with the dumbstruck adults and a slither of Thomas the Tank Engine served on a plate which looked like a reject from a utility crockery set, our Lone Entertainer disappeared into the night, just missing his tall head on our low door frame. 'Gee, and I wanted to thank him.'

The Archbishop has a way with children, natural, not so much coming down to their level as raising them up to his. He avoids the silly patronizing voice that most adults reserve for children. He does not bombard them with activity and talk. He just attends to them as equals and so disarmingly wins their confidence.

On another occasion, at a Palace Christmas party, our children were enraptured as their Archbishop crawled and growled across the floor, introducing them to his tiger. Ever since the tiger has remained Hannah's favourite animal, and I am not at all surprised. The mitred tiger, habitat by the Ouse, is the rarest and loveliest cat of them all. Better even than Little Luke, whoever he may be.

17 JANUARY

Two schools to visit today. A morning call at a local authority primary school to celebrate its centenary. The school should have been rehoused long ago, since the place is far too small for the children, let alone for the parents who have crammed in. The Victorian windows are high, well above the children's eye-level, denying them the pleasures of the countryside beyond. And the place is draughty; secondary double glazing would be impossible with frames of that shape and size.

We robe in the nearby village hall, then process across the busy main road, the Archbishop acting as a lollipop man with his crosier and holding up the startled traffic.

A substandard school building does not make for a substandard school. In fact the deficiencies of the building were set in sharp contrast to the prevailing atmosphere, which had a distinct family feel to it. This family was whole enough to laugh at itself, to recall its ups and downs without malice, to affirm each other irrespective of potential and ability. The school's size meant that no one could avoid each other—we literally had to rub shoulders crammed into such a small space. And that seemed to have bequeathed the warm accepted feel which the Archbishop was quick to draw on in his jolly little talk, just *having* to get on with each other because we were so close together. Still, I could have done without the crosier in such cramped conditions; even a generous spirit is severely tested when he keeps being prodded by a crook.

Later that afternoon we visited a public school which was as well-equipped as our morning school had been ill-equipped. Lavish gym facilities, a heated swimming-pool, spacious classrooms, a plush chapel. The pupils and staff however were standoffish and difficult to engage in conversation. Clipped noes and yeses were all you could get out of them. They seemed uninterested in one another and in you. Our visit culminated with a Eucharist for which we had strict instructions. These specifically stressed that the Peace was *never* shared between members of the congregation.

'Well, "never" ends with our visit,' I quipped to the Archbishop as we mugged up on our orders beforehand.

He was unsympathetic. 'No, when in Rome we'll do as the Romans. And we can't have boys at a public school being encouraged to touch each other.'

Two schools. One wanting for nothing, where its pupils were so isolated from each other that they were forbidden to shake hands. The other wanting for everything but love and acceptance. I felt God was giving us a parable again.

To begin your Confirmation sermon with the words, 'Yesterday I was engrossed in conversation with an IRA terrorist' certainly makes for an arresting start, especially if you take into account the predominantly traditional right-wing congregation the Archbishop was addressing. But the ruse certainly grabbed their attention and ultimately won their sympathy as the story was unpacked. The terrorist had come to faith while in prison, had repented of his former violence, and was resolved to make a new start. The whole episode was seen as a paradigm of the conversion which all the candidates, in their own way, were celebrating that night.

And the reasons those candidates had come to this point were multifarious. Most touching was the story of a young couple who knelt together before the Archbishop. The husband was thickset, with the gait and broken nose of a former rugby player mediated by a certain joviality. His wife in contrast was of slight build and beautiful in a frail sort of way. They made a good couple; and yet there was an aura of sadness about them.

The reason for this became clear afterwards. The woman had recently given birth prematurely at home. The newborn baby had died, gasping for breath, in her arms, with her husband looking on, just minutes before medical help had arrived. Through the inevitable contact with their local church through the days and weeks that followed something had touched them and had brought them to this night. In the midst of such utter tragedy, faith had grown. It seemed supremely fitting that the Archbishop was there both to bless their continuing pilgrimage and to cradle their sorrow.

They were not the only ones to be ministered to that night. For many others the penny seemed to have dropped and their lives were clearly and irrevocably changed for ever. It was a magic night, not in the pagan sense, but in a Christian sense, akin to that childhood experience when all seems to stand still as Christmas Eve waits for Christmas Day's dawn.

Not that it was all so intense. At the bunfight afterwards I overheard the Archbishop's conversation with an elderly couple. The man was a retired scratch farmer, with a wiry, lean frame, yet taut with energy. His wife's figure, in contrast, was bell-shaped. 'I hope you feed yourselves properly in your retirement,' the Archbishop asked in a concerned tone. 'For instance, tell me what you have for your lunch!'

The bell-shaped woman responded, 'Ee, your Grace, we often have fresh air.'

'Fresh air? Fresh air?' the Archbishop exclaimed, his eyebrows rising in proportion to his concern. 'You need something more sustaining than that.'

The woman and her husband were clearly nonplussed. 'What could be better than fresh 'are? He goes out and shoots it at dawn and then I boils it up for our dinner. You get a tidy bit of meat of a doe.' The Archbishop made a strategic withdrawal, one culture saluting another in passing.

3 FEBRUARY

Every so often we have a big do in the Minster to consecrate a bishop. It is a 24-hour affair, beginning with the rehearsal after Evensong the night before. The bishops-elect, trying to prove themselves holy men, always attend Choral Evensong with great piety, so I have to lurk by the Screen Door after the service has ended and pick my man. From time to time I nobble the wrong one, and some rustic cleric innocently enjoying a visit to town garnished with Evensong suddenly finds greatness almost thrust upon him.

The new bishops usually stand out like a sore thumb, however. Well dressed, with wives and families in dutiful attendance, all attempting to be what I term 'terminally pastoral', the sort of explicit concern, head tilted at exactly the correct compassionate degree, that makes their victim want to shrivel up and die. Fortunately the phase soon wears off and the bishops' humour and natural skills shine through once again.

The rehearsal is akin to trying to drive a fast car with several people battling over the steering wheel, which has just come off. The bishops-elect, already hyped up into a management mode, try to direct. The Precentor tries to direct, but is far too kind, resorting to clapping his hands at intervals and shrieking 'Gentlemen, please!' like a cross between Frankie Howerd and Kenneth Williams. I try to direct, a mere David amongst all these Goliaths; one day my stone will come.

At my first ever consecration, the Archbishop tried to direct (he leaves it to me now) but was thwarted by the funniest bishop I have ever encountered. The Archbishop duly rehearsed his line, 'I, John, Primate of England,' but was interrupted by a loud guffaw.

'Primate, Primate—it makes you sound like an ape!' The Archbishop gave an icy stare: he was not amused. But the bishop-to-be was not to be cowed and continued with his wisecracks. He is still laughing four years later, his sense of humour uneroded by the tedium of episcopacy. Which is just as well, since laughter is at the very heart of God, even if it is conspicuously lacking in his Church.

Following the frustrations of rehearsal comes the procession by car through York's maze of a one-way system to dinner and overnight stay at Bishopthorpe. The new bishops, usually having had their new car delivered that day, and prone to stop for and beam at every pedestrian who shows the slightest inkling of wanting to cross the road, are sluggish drivers to say the least. I lead, keep them in my mirror and try desperately hard not to lose any of them or gain any gatecrashers. On one memorable occasion I had to pull up three times and go in search of the lost shepherd.

Having duly arrived, dinner and polite conversation follow with a game of snooker for the youngsters whilst the Archbishop takes the new boys aside and tells them the episcopal facts of life, like a dutiful mother enlightening a blushing bride on her wedding eve. 'You have to do *what* with your crosier?! I never dreamt for one moment . . .'

A sleepless night is followed all too soon by morning with boiled eggs for breakfast and Mattins in chapel. Joking apart, I invariably find this quiet service, as these men humbly prepare to make a massive step, the most numinous of the whole day. I pray,

> What is soiled, make thou pure;
> What is wounded, work its cure;
> What is parched, fructify;
> What is rigid, gently bend;
> What is frozen, warmly tend;
> Strengthen what goes erringly.

I mean it with all my heart and soul. Only too aware of the real sacrifice that awaits them, their people expectant of unstinting and brilliant service, I am all too often moved to tears.

That sense of thrill is retained for the two-hour consecration.

The full Minster; the rousing hymns; the Archbishop intoning each word perfectly; the red-robed bishops crowded round the Archbishop, hands held out in assistance as he ordains; the wave of applause as the new bishops process out with their Archbishop at the end: images that will remain for a lifetime.

The service is followed by a scrumptious lunch for the existing bishops and wives, with the new bishops being presented with the sweet. All a bit like a wedding: 'Now, this is your Uncle Carlisle, your Auntie Blackburn, your cousin, Chester . . .' And as at every wedding your spirits soar and you look forward to the next time.

7 FEBRUARY

To a Midlands mining village to celebrate a minuscule church's one-hundred-and-fiftieth. The peal of bells was a recording (set at the wrong speed, I fear), the vestry was the bedroom of an adjacent bungalow, with all the attentions of its aged owner, who employed an 'OAP' to cut her grass!

The predominant accent was surprisingly West Country. The church was full of flowers with colour schemes unashamedly mismatched. Most hideous of all was a baby doll, squatting in the font as if it were a potty.

The organist had MS, but played beautifully, with a serene smile which belied the ravages of his disease. At the end of the service he struggled painfully through the crowds to the back of the church to greet the Archbishop. Gospel images leapt to mind; someone taking a photograph flashed us back into the present.

Everyone was so thrilled the Archbishop had come, and gave him rapt attention. His sermon (as well as drawing our attentions to the deprivations of the mid-nineteenth century) focused on Archbishop Harcourt who consecrated the church one hundred and fifty years before in his eighty-sixth year! That Archbishop had been quite a character: sixteen children, legal wrangles over deposing the Dean, finally dying of pneumonia in his ninety-second year after frightening frogs by falling in the lake. The aged Harcourt had visited the place because small places and people matter to God, the present and youthful Archbishop stressed. God's name and heart and eyes are in this place; eyes watching, seeing through, accepting. A true church gives people the freedom to articulate their faith in familiar words and be themselves before God.

13 FEBRUARY

The snow had fallen heavily all night long, transforming the grounds into a winter wonderland. Wet snow decorated all the trees, bowing their branches in homage. Countless creatures had left their prints: a marauding fox; a flustered pheasant; a scavenging squirrel, its buried treasure lost for a time; a rabbit, whose flurry meant snow lay scattered around its tracks. All ye ice and snow, bless ye the Lord . . .

The scene inevitably draws you to worship. The Palace chapel is basked in a strange light for an early Eucharist, celebrated by me with the Archbishop and Raymond Barker in the congregation; when two or three are gathered together . . .

Celebrating Communion here never ceases to make me feel both immensely privileged and also immensely unworthy. Celebrating our Lord's Supper anywhere is awesome enough, but here you are additionally a-tremble at the one who is in the congregation and his predecessors who haunt us. The legend goes that when the champion of the Reformation, Martin Luther, first celebrated communion after his break with Rome, with arguments over transubstantiation, consubstantiation, and any-substantiation raging like fires, he shook with fear, so much so that he dropped a host as he administered and no one dared pick it up. I know the feeling.

I was strictly trained at a popular Cambridge college to avoid such accidents when administering. For instance, we were taught never to let the chalice go but always to co-hold it with the communicant. The reason was that years before a West Indian lady, a Hot Gospel devotee, had grabbed the chalice at the rail and tipped the contents over her head, proclaiming, 'I's been washed in the blood of the Lamb.'

Ever since, I have dutifully held tightly onto the chalice, with one exception. I always let it go for John Habgood, for two reasons. First, his track record leads me to conclude he is extremely unlikely to ape the behaviour of our West Indian lady. Second, even if he were to surprise us, I somehow sense the blood of the Lamb would not be far from home.

I know it is a strange thing to love, but I love the Vale of York, madly, truly, deeply. Madly, because it is flat and boring and unworthy of sane attention. Truly, because only here do I feel that this is home, where I was born to be. Deeply, because I pore over the Ordnance Survey map of the area as if it is the most sacred Scripture.

So today was a moving pilgrimage for me indeed, a confirmation at the heart of the Vale. The church was by the Derwent, half a mile from the village, reached by a rugged, muddy path. The car had been abandoned long ago and we trudged the way, the hems of our cassocks the hue of black mud.

The church was pretty: a squat Tudor tower, a Norman nave, a dogtooth chancel arch, a tiny chancel. In the silences of the service you could hear the dark waters lapping against the churchyard's west wall; in winter, the Derwent is in perpetual flood and turns low meadowland, known locally as ings, into a veritable Lake District. The music from the wheezy harmonium was supplemented with the haunting call of Russian geese, flying overhead. When the organ mercifully shut up, I could hear their wings beating against the night air.

'Come thou Holy Spirit, come,' the organ droned out, joined by a few discordant voices. The water lapping, the birds calling, the wings beating: the Spirit which breathed over the abyss had indeed come.

Which is more than one of the confirmation candidates. There were only two to begin with: hardly an evangelistic success story. Then one had dropped out, with no explanation, simply not turning up. The service's start had been delayed whilst we waited. The vicar to-ed and fro-ed to the porch, peering into the dark night, willing her to come. 'She'll just be putting the children to bed; she'll be along in a minute.' And then, 'Her husband's rather difficult; perhaps she's cajoling him to come with her.' And finally, 'Oh dear, oh dear, she's not coming. We'd better start without her.' The voice full of sadness; all the encouragement, all the patient instruction come to naught.

The vicar's sadness was matched by the Archbishop. No recrimination, no 'You haven't done your job very well, have you?' Just a void, an ache, shared between vicar and Archbishop, two men who shared the cure of souls in that place.

At least there was still one candidate. A little plump girl in her best party frock, who dangled her legs self-consciously and stared around vacantly as the Archbishop preached.

And so the service came to its end. Great expectations, great hopes, but a sorry stillbirth. De la Mare came to mind with his '"Tell them I came and no one answered, that I kept my word," he said.' We packed our cases, trudged back over the stony path and left the church behind, its dark stones silhouetted against the clear starlit sky. The lapping water and beating wings waited for the next time.

I did warn him. I am used to schools: talking to primary children I enjoy; talking to secondary pupils I dread. They are so bolshie at that age, and anyone in a clerical collar is a soft target for their cruel taunts. So I *knew* that the Archbishop's talk to the sixth form would be no pushover. But he would have none of it. 'David, just show a little more enthusiasm, if you please.' So I shut up. I had read that Douglas Hurd, another Etonian, had flogged fags for showing 'insufficient enthusiasm', so I did not want to share their fate. John Habgood was a convincing servant of Christ, but the patrician still lurked beneath the surface.

It was the sixth form biology class which was our target. The *crème de la crème* of that class sang in the school choir and had been withdrawn to rehearse for that afternoon's service, leaving about twenty others. The purple-cassocked Archbishop bustled in, flanked by a proud but nervous Head, willing everything to go all right. 'Good morning, 6S,' he intoned, 'This is the Archbishop of York.'

The youngsters could not have been more stunned had their Head introduced a live diplodocus into the classroom. It was clear they had never seen the likes of this bespectacled creature, complete with purple dress, ever before. So the Archbishop had to take the initiative and break the pregnant silence: 'Good morning. I've not always been the Archbishop of York. I used to be a scientist and like you studied science in the sixth form.'

This statement, rather than reassuring them, really blew their minds. There was just the remotest chance they might have encountered the Church of England before, and a little explanation might have enlightened them as to what an Archbishop was about. But a man in a purple frock who was really a scientist was clearly totally beyond belief.

But the Archbishop was not to be deterred. 'Now I'm sure

some of you are studying biology because you want to be a scientist. Am I right?' The ensuing silence made it all too clear that he was definitely wrong.

He tried a different tack. 'Any of you going to read biology at university?' The sound of silence was unabated.

'Well, let me tell you about what I did at university,' the Archbishop continued, diplomatically not mentioning Eton or Cambridge. Even he was beginning to flag. 'I studied Pharmacology and Physiology. Anybody know what these two subjects are about?' The biology teacher looked nonplussed, let alone the class.

'Let me tell you.' The Archbishop answered his own question, since clearly no one else was going to. 'The two subjects look at how a body responds to certain stimuli and medication. It was truly fascinating. I experimented on dead frogs (Animal Liberation Movement please note) and myself to see how organisms react to pain.'

The Archbishop was in his stride now, as he reminisced over his Cambridge days: 'Do you know, I once ate a pound of salt to see what it did to my blood pressure. Another time I spent a week eating nothing but porridge and monitored all my excreta to see what effect it had.'

The look was the same on each of the faces of those sixth formers, which said, 'This man is seriously insane.'

The Archbishop obviously got the message and decided to make a run for it whilst the going was good. 'Well, I mustn't interrupt your studies any more. It's been good meeting you all. I wish you every success with your future.' And with that he beat it. I did not say a word; I did not have to.

Before the school commemoration service the vicar served an absolutely delicious lunch, which was a tremendous aid to recovery. The Archbishop was animated in conversation, so animated that as he gesticulated the flap of his jacket landed in the middle of the trifle on a nearby table. The result was that he was going around oblivious to the generous portion of cream on his jacket-back. Obviously no one would ever dare to say to an archbishop, let alone this one, 'Archbishop, you've got some cream on your back.' Eventually I bit the bullet and whispered to him in a quiet moment. He gave me an accusing look, as if I had been spraying whipped cream around. The messenger of bad news always carries the blame.

The service went brilliantly, with bands and choirs galore. The Archbishop impressed the congregation of youngsters and their parents with a sensitive sermon, all too aware of the current educational scene. I resolved that in the future we would stick to pulpits and avoid sixth forms.

11 MARCH

The British Armed Forces' main activity these days is to keep the peace, a senior officer emphasized to me. That somewhat jarred with the soldiers who guarded the entrance to the army college and pointed their machine guns at us threateningly. Gordon, an ex-Regimental Sergeant Major, soon sorted them out with crisp tones which would have put the fear of God into God and they apologetically let us through. I always thought the British Army pretty big; not big enough, though, for Gordon not to know virtually every soldier.

The service was to mark the graduation of several hundred army cadets. They were all arrayed before the Archbishop and stood, sat, and knelt to attention. The Archbishop preached on a competition between the world's rivers, but unfortunately got his Mississippis confused with his Amazons, a rash mistake if you are planning an invasion. Eventually he settled on the Nile as his paradigm of something which watered the desert and made it green, a striking feature as you flew over Africa, as cadets are wont. That was precisely the role of these new soldiers, to nourish those places in which they served, to turn deserts and wildernesses into pasturage.

I am sure that if John Habgood became a soldier, that is the honourable way he would play it. I was less sure, however, that these soldiers were capable of becoming John Habgoods. That I felt was the Archbishop's fatal flaw when he passed comment on limited strikes and peacekeeping forces, in that he seemed to take insufficient account of the sheer momentum of resentment, frustration, and raw need for revenge which would drive lesser men than him into losing their cool.

Memories of the day? We were well and warmly looked after. When we go on tour people recognize the Archbishop and know what he is about; they are bewildered by me, since they have not really got a clue as to what an Archbishop's chaplain does, and look even more puzzled when I explain. More often than not if we are visiting a church people ask if I am the vicar, which says mountains about their involvement. For my part, my heart sinks every time we walk into each reception, since I have to sell myself from rest. But it wasn't like that with the army; they had me marked out as an ADC to my ecclesiastical general *par excellence*, and linked me with my military equivalents; it was all tremendously relaxed and I felt grateful for their care.

Other memories are less happy. The tea and biscuits in the drill hall afterwards with the heavy fog of cigarette smoke as nearly every candidate lit up. And the girls, only sixteen going on seventeen, now allowed in the army as equals, with heavy boots and khaki kit, already brutalized by the system. And if, as I quite rightly felt, *they* should not be brutalized, then no one should be brutalized.

19 MARCH

A busy day: a confirmation in the morning, a lunch to open a new hospice with a celebration in a nearby church following. The confirmation was a high church affair, successfully stage-managed by a new deacon keen to impress us with his efficiency. But for all the ritual, the occasion was relaxed, with the Archbishop preaching on perseverance—'I've started so I'll finish . . .' I fear the *Mastermind* allusion was lost on the poor folk who made up the bulk of the congregation. We later heard of a candidate's mother who was unavoidably absent due to breaking her foot when falling out of bed drunk.

The candidates were presented by their godparents or relatives which was a distinctly nice touch. All were anointed, although one forgot to remain kneeling and had to return for a second attempt, any embarrassment dissipated by a tender smile from the Archbishop. The hymns were all drawn from *English Hymnal* (very unrevised) and were lovely and quaint; healthily there was no infestation by *Mission Praise*. The abiding memory is of rows and rows of the congregation genuflecting as the Archbishop passed by and blessed them. A happy visit.

Finding the hospice was no easy task. Initially we went down a wrong corridor and ended up in a geriatric hospital. The nursing staff looked the cassocked Archbishop and chaplain up and down with great suspicion. Had I had my wits about me, I would have exclaimed in my best Geordie accent, 'Ee, luv, I found this old geezer wandering about outside dressed only in this purple nightie. You want to be more careful and lock them in . . .' But there again, I rather like my job.

SPRING

Sometimes my mind is distracted and I fail to notice or be alert, which for a Benedictine soul like mine is a great sin. Today was such a day, although there were mitigating circumstances. The journey to the Tyne went by in a haze. The church we arrived at was a modern, redbrick building, but I recall no further detail than that. The congregation was mostly elderly, although encouragingly there were a few young mums with lively offspring. The service went OK with no major blunders.

The reason why my memory is so scant is because I was worried. The Archbishop sat at the entrance to the sanctuary beneath a massive cross which must have been 12 ft in span (4 m in Eurospeak), suspended from the ceiling. On the cross was an equally massive Jesus, who was dressed as a Palestinian peasant, although the pink head-dress made him look effeminate despite his hulking size.

The cross was suspended by thin, almost invisible wire at an angle which made Jesus look very threatening, as if he were going to swoop over the congregation in a sort of celestial and judgemental fly-past. The whole construction did not look at all safe; in fact it looked positively dangerous. For the entire service I was so concerned that the whole thing might fall on the Archbishop that sheer terror blocked out awareness of anything else. I was willing the thing to stay put.

Mind you, worried though I was about losing my boss in such tragic circumstances, I suppose having Jesus fall on top of you is an apt if novel way for an Archbishop to go. Even so, a Jesus with a pink head-dress?!

'Tiptoe through the tulips . . .' Not tulips but daffodils, and Farndale daffodils at that, a small variety of daffodil which in springtime carpets the dale on the North York Moors where it is indigenous. Since they are a protected species we had to walk through them very gingerly; the offence of crushing a daffodil still carries capital punishment in these parts.

Our walk began in Farndale's tiny church with the blessing of the daffodils. It's rather touching to think that the architect of the Act of Synod, amongst many other things, has time to pause and bless flowers. Even though the dale seemed sparsely populated, the church was packed with locals, who presumably lived in caves like trogs since there certainly were not enough dwellings to house them. Mercifully we were on the wrong side of the Pennines to have Wordsworth's poem read out. Even then the Archbishop found the subject of daffodils an irresistible one for his sermon, focusing on their ephemeral beauty to draw analogies with the transitory nature of our own lives.

Then came the muddy walk along the beck side, the high hills of Farndale overshadowing us. The tiny distinctive Farndale daffodils were all around us, but were not all that profuse; not a patch on our yellow carpet at Bishopthorpe or for that matter around York's city walls. But there again, the Archbishop did say they were ephemeral; perhaps they had taken offence and decided their day had gone.

10 APRIL

Every Holy Week the Senior Staff of the York Diocese celebrate the Via Dolorosa of Jesus by going away together for a 24-hour silent retreat at Parceval Hall, a plush retreat house nestling in Wharfedale. I am well accustomed to living in a silent if mobile order; the other members of the Senior Staff are less so, and the strain soon begins to tell.

The highlight of the twenty-four hours are the four addresses delivered by a celebrity, who despite being flanked by these ecclesiastical heavyweights, never appears in the least bit nervous. The food is superb, although one does feel a few pangs of guilt as you think of the trial of the one who hungered and thirsted after righteousness at this time.

Different members of the Senior Staff do different things. Some read the newspapers in minute detail even down to the financial sections. Others snatch a learned theological tome from the library shelves and smile and nod sagely, giving themselves away by doing so at the wrong points. Some are past pretending; they snuggle down in a comfortable corner and enjoy *The Rector's Wife*. Some take to their beds and snooze. Coming across a pyjamaed George Austin stumbling along the corridor in the middle of the afternoon makes me grateful, for once, that the company is not mixed.

One year the Archbishop and I coincided with our choice of books. John V. Taylor's *The Christlike God* is a firework display of a book and deserves repeated reading. Since we were working our way through the same material I decided to check the Archbishop's reading speed against mine. I chalked up a pretty mean thirty pages an hour. I timed the Archbishop from my vantage point in a shady nook. His time put mine to shame—thirty-six seconds a page, or one hundred pages an hour. I definitely played tortoise to his hare, although I gained a distinct advantage when he nodded off in the evening whilst I plodded on.

For me the hills beckon, although so far I have never succeeded in enticing any other member of the Senior Staff to join me. Simon's Seat (a very appropriate destination in a Holy Week which stars Simon Peter so much) is the peak of Wharfedale, and presents an invigorating and often treacherous climb. Simultaneously the worst and the best year was when I climbed it in a thick mist, checking I was on the right path by the sole criterion that, like Jesus forty days after Easter, I had to be ascending. For the last hundred yards I fumbled and felt my way along slippery rocks covered with lichen and miraculously found the trig point. I sat there in the chilly fog, getting my breath back, basking in the eeriness of it all. And then all at once the cloud blew away, so that only wisps remained. I saw Wharfedale's panorama in all its sunny splendour. Moments later the mist returned, but that one glimpse of glory made it all so worthwhile.

The retreat addresses are a highlight but not *the* highlight. That accolade has to fall to the climb and all it says about the faith: to struggle on through the mist to be fuelled by the glimpses of glory on the mountain top. Some weeks later, an earnest American cornered me (a Southern Baptist), looked me straight in the eye, and asked, 'David, what experience of spiritual renewal have you had in Yorkshire?'

I looked back at him, unrattled by an inquisitiveness and intrusiveness which assumed an air of superiority and replied, 'I have to say I find the Dales very refreshing.' I guess that was not quite the answer he was hankering after, but I meant it with all my heart.

15 APRIL

Services mean different things to different people. For some, the Easter Vigil in York Minster, beginning in absolute darkness and ending in light, is a moving celebration of a Resurrection about to break, a Tomb about to empty. For others, as the celebration moves into the crypt for baptism and confirmation by the Archbishop, the hairs on the backs of their necks stand up as they realize that on this very spot on this very Eve in AD 627, Bishop Paulinus baptized King Edwin and made York Christian—for a while. York has been Christian on and off ever since.

For me, the service involves more mundane things. For a start, there is the heavy primatial cross, difficult enough to carry in the light and so absolutely treacherous in the dark. Fortunately I do not have to hold the thing for the entire proceedings: there is a clasp on the side of the Archbishop's chair which I can place it in. However, finding the clasp in the dark is another matter, since you either score first time or give up. One year the clasp had for some reason migrated from the Archbishop's right side to his left. I thought of feeling around him in the darkness but on reflection I decided against; he might get the wrong idea.

Halfway through the Vigil the whole congregation processes down some steep and lethal steps, definitely off-piste, into the tiny crypt, with low, vaulted, stone ceiling. The whole exercise is an ecclesiastical version of that 1960's fad, 'How many people can you get into a Mini?' with the steps an added bonus. How we end up without any injury constantly amazes me. But we never have so much as a scratch. The scrum assemble, candles in hand, faces yellow in the candlelight, and the atmosphere is terrific, if a little warm.

One year I thought I had tumbled down the steps, since I was definitely suffering the effects of concussion, seeing not double but triple. The Archbishop was baptizing triplets in the tiny font recessed into the wall. The recess was not made for a tall man complete with mitre, so to get the baby anywhere near the water is a considerable achievement. To do that three times is near miraculous. Baptizing triplets down there was a first for the Minster, as was the triplets' mother's insistence that she retain her maiden name in the baptism register that went back centuries.

Baptism and confirmation over, we totter out of the crypt and breathe a sigh of relief. 'Christ is risen. He is risen indeed, alleluia!' He must be risen if he can protect so many of his followers doing such foolhardy things. After all, even Jesus had the tomb to himself. He did not have to share it with two hundred candle-wielding enthusiasts, complete with triplets.

23 APRIL

Once a year the Archbishop invites all the ordinands in his diocese to tea in his home *en masse*. About seventy usually turn up for a fun-packed afternoon which includes a lecture, discussion, a scrumptious tea rounded off with that well-known cure for indigestion, Evensong. Like the law of the Medes and Persians, the programme has remained unchanged through the years. It is the same format I attended in my youth, the same format attended by my father in his youth, and so on, from generation to generation. And it works.

Over the years we have had speakers of quality whose message has soaked into the soul and left one warmly contented. The Archbishop is attentive, and draws out the speaker's points so that everyone can appreciate their significance. Unlike the headmaster who felt it was his divine right to summarize my assemblies: I was constantly surprised that whatever I said could be condensed into either an admonition about not running in corridors or using only one paper towel at a time. The Archbishop listens, absorbs, and then re-expresses the subtleties.

David Konstant, the Roman Catholic Bishop of Leeds, spoke revealingly about how they selected priests the RC way, which seemed to involve a rigorous selection process whose findings were then chiefly ignored. 'Twenty-seven out of thirty results are wrong,' the Bishop quipped.

'Twenty-seven out of thirty of ours are right,' the Archbishop rejoindered. He would say that, wouldn't he, since he had to uphold the system with all his ordinands gathered before him. And yet what he said was also true. In our diocese the selection process includes affirmation by the candidate's parish, meeting with a local clergyperson experienced in the issue of vocation, several searching interviews with me, four long references taken up, and an intimidating interview with the local bishop. Then the Archbishop himself goes through the candidate's file and decides whether to sponsor or not to sponsor for the dreaded selection conference. Not the tiniest detail escapes his searing gaze.

The conference itself consists of a series of exercises and interviews where the nervous candidate is thrown in at the deep end. Some claim this to be grossly unfair. Yet ordained ministry is often on the frontiers in unknown situations. Although I have taken hundreds of funerals I have yet to approach the bereaved family without my stomach churning with nerves. How a nervous candidate functions at a selection conference speaks mountains about performance in the nervous climes of ordained ministry.

Those who are not recommended go through an inevitable bereavement process, akin to a stillbirth where hope has been so savagely dashed. My job as Director of Ordinands is to stay with them, hear their grief, but also to stay with what the conference says about them, so that in time they can hear it and discover a new direction to which God may be calling them.

It is all serious stuff. Conversations on Ordinands' Day are about big issues, life and death issues, and I am privileged to witness the many and varied ways Gods has touched them. Listening to them drives me to ponder anew my own vocation.

David Konstant's visit sticks in my mind not primarily because of his talk, good though that was, but for an incident which happened beforehand. The three of us were in the entrance hall before the others arrived, talking about this and that when we were interrupted by a call. It was a young woman's voice shouting from the Archbishop's quarters the single word, 'Dad!' The Archbishop made his apologies and left to respond to his daughter.

I felt immensely sad to know that was a word which David Konstant would never hear addressed to him. And behind that single word was a whole world of love and tears, joys and frustrations, expectations and disappointments, a whole school of life which had clearly made our Archbishop and was equally clearly denied his Roman Catholic counterpart. It would be impertinent of me to trespass on the Archbishop's family life other than to say he comes across as a tender husband and father, cherishing and cherished by his family. I grieved that such a lovely man as David Konstant was denied that.

Tender family man the Archbishop undoubtedly is; tender with his chaplain always he ain't! I work hard for Ordinands' Day, co-ordinating the tea, liaising with the speaker, ordering and printing the service, chatting with the ordinands, having mugged up on their details beforehand. By the end I feel happily exhausted. After one of the most successful ordinands' days of my time, the Archbishop's sole comment was about the altar candles in chapel, which had burnt out during the service. 'You're getting meaner with those candles; you should have replaced them; it wasn't a good example to set.'

I recalled a church garden party which had gone with a swing. The sun had shone, the band had played, the stalls had sold out, profits broke all records. Everyone was delighted. Nearly everyone. One old man marched up to the vicar and pointed an accusing finger at him, 'Now tell me, what would you have done if it had rained?' There's always one.

Becoming a Licensed woman (or man) is perhaps not every Christian's dream even if it is their private fantasy. Yet for a priest or layworker to operate at all, they need a licence. And so every six months a gaggle of new appointees comes to Bishopthorpe Chapel to be duly authorized by the Archbishop.

You can tell it is Licensing Day by the straggle of licensees and their supporters timidly making their way up the drive, like fledgling sheepdogs, cautiously exploring new territory. The Palace is built so that as you walk towards it you are faced by about twenty massive windows. Already nervous, you feel that some-one is watching you out of each and every one of them, weighing you in the balance and finding you wanting. I know how all eyes of the Bishopthorpe synagogue seem fixed on you, so I try desperately hard to put visitors at their ease. I am not helped by the cold reception area, a piece of sixties architecture with BHS lights, wedged in between the lavatories and the entrance hall. A fireplace stands chillingly empty with what appears to be a skull on the mantelpiece. If you are not nervous to start with, you certainly are after sitting in there for five minutes.

However, today I greet people at the door, show the new ministers where to robe, show their guests into chapel, and then the fun begins. Bewigged Registrar precedes robed Archbishop who precedes lowly chaplain. The whole event has the stuff of intense boredom about it which drives me to distraction.

The Archbishop begins, 'We John, by Divine Provid-ence . . .'

('And by the Crown Appointments' Commission,' I silently add.)

'. . . Lord Archbishop of York in the twelfth year of our translation . . .'

('How do you translate Archbishop of York into German?' I muse.)

'. . . to our beloved in Christ . . .'
(Kiss, kiss.)
'. . . greetings . . .'

All that preamble for a greeting! And so it goes on and on. Oaths are sworn on a New Testament containing the words of the one who prohibited any oaths, obedience is sworn to the Queen and her heirs (allowed to proceed to the throne by divine permission of the Archdeacon of York) and to the Archbishop and his successors ('I wonder who that'll be?') in all things lawful and honest. (I start composing a list of things illegal and dishonest that archbishops are wont to do, but come up with nothing.) Then, with a quick dash through the Lord's Prayer (old version inevitably) the whole thing comes to its end. Boring but mercifully quite brief. The new ministers are now duly licensed and can run amok.

Actually, the Archbishop lightens the whole proceedings. The twinkle in his eye and the deep awe in his voice are enough to make the dry momentous. He links the legal process with the need for tradition, for handing down the faith, for honouring the riches of the past.

The Victorian stained-glass windows he uses as visual aids (he is mercifully allergic to flip charts) depict a highly romanticized version of how Christianity came to a pagan North, which suffered and endured attack by missionaries on two fronts— Gregory, Augustine, and Paulinus from the South, and Columba and Aidan from the North.

Edwin beams at us as an example of what Christianity can do for a king. Hilda has a place as the ultimate reconciler of the northern and southern brands of Christianity, which formerly were so divided that they celebrated Easter on two different dates; once is exhausting enough! Mind you, since Hilda is also famous for founding an abbey on the inhospitable climes of Whitby's chill south cliff, her powers of decision-making and discernment seem to me to be highly questionable. Bede gains a place because he was that ultimate of ecclesiastical gossips, scriptwriting the whole epic.

Everyone leaves the chapel not only licensed but also

educated, athirst for refreshment. Tea is a great event. A cuppa served by Mrs Habgood with posh biscuits galore absolutely thrills the visitors. Downtown Middlesbrough stands alongside upper-suburb York, prison warder stands alongside public schoolmaster, coalminer stands alongside bank manager, all getting on famously. A wonderful Kingdom mix enabled by the Archbishop's generous hospitality.

30 APRIL

As a schoolboy I often used to walk down Coney Street in York, and enjoyed its hustle and bustle tremendously. Nothing could beat it on a winter's evening, the bright lights blazing: Terry's restaurant and chocolate shop at the end; the vans to-ing and fro-ing to the *Evening Press* offices; Leek and Thorpe's, a department store *par excellence*. Jutting out across the street was this massive clock, attached to St Martin le Grand. It had stopped when the church had been bombed in the Baedecker raids during the last war. That for me gave the clock great poignancy, a wounded soldier driving you to remember.

Now Coney Street is only a shadow of its former self, and I miss it all so. The *Evening Press* has moved out, Leek and Thorpe's has been hacked to pieces, Terry's restaurant has closed, leaving you at the mercy of Betty's, across the road. And worst of all, the clock has been restored and started again. No longer poignant, no longer a reminder, except of the right time in a world obsessed with the right time.

And so it was that with a heavy heart I accompanied the Archbishop to mark twenty-five years since St Martin's restoration. That restoration was remarkable: George Pace at his best, hanging lights, black supports, bare bulbs, lots of white oak, filtering the light and somehow making it brighter, as a contrast to the darkness of war. On one stone is a simple inscription: Father Forgive 1939–1945. Not, as some American tourists thought, a memorial to a previous incumbent, but a heartfelt plea for a healing of atrocities.

We were badly wrong-footed. Still half a mile from the church we came across hoards and hoards of marching Scouts, parading in the opposite direction from the way we wanted to go. There was no alternative but to abandon Gordon and the car and hoof it, robe cases under each arm, going against the flow of drum majorettes with their interminable tunes which assailed us.

Once in the church I realized we had the wrong set of robes. The vicar had assured me it was to be Choral Evensong when in fact it turned out to be Solemn Evensong. To the world at large, one evensong may seem very much like another; but in the narrow confines of the Church, Choral equals choir and therefore dictates choir dress whereas Solemn equals incense which naturally dictates copes.

With Gordon marooned half a mile away we had to wear the only robes we had available. I felt so self-conscious, scarf-and-hooded chaplain following rochet-and-chimered Archbishop, with incense wafting all around, like Paisleyite protesters at a Papal Mass. I suppose it was a way of getting my own back because they had started the clock.

3 MAY

Our 8.0 a.m. start was delayed by a problem with ducks. Since the Archbishop and his wife are very fond of them, perplexity abounded when a duck and her fluffy ducklings seemed in great distress on the Palace drive. A gang of eight drakes were all trying to cover her simultaneously and separate her from her offspring. Archbishop and chaplain came to her rescue, scattering her suitors whilst driving her back towards her chicks. The vision of the Archbishop galloping down the drive, clapping with each step, drakes fearfully taking flight over the clock tower, stayed with me all day. Not for nothing is his nickname the Saviour.

Our destination was Whitehaven, over the A66 and Bowes Moor, then around Penrith to the Northern Lakes, their hills surrounded by halos of mist. We stopped by Bassenthwaite to share my flask of coffee, Skiddaw and Catbells keeping us company. 'I love climbing these hills with our girls,' I informed the Archbishop, to break our silence. 'What about you? Do you climb here?'

'Not any more,' the Archbishop curtly replied. Considering the way he shot up the stairs at the Palace, I was surprised. 'I remember coming to Keswick for the Convention in 1947, though.'

Now that did surprise me. One year our Lake District holiday had coincided with the Keswick Convention, and I remember the Convention Tent disgorging its hoards of an evening. I found it frightening since they all looked so similar: staring eyes, fixed smiles, *Good News Bibles* clutched under their arm. The Archbishop had clearly climbed a long way from these origins.

We dropped into Whitehaven after a further hour's drive to the partially restored church at the centre, all tower and transept. One of the many worthy people to whom we were introduced remains with me. A Sri Lankan priest, wheelchair-bound, recovering from surgery to remove a massive brain tumour. The Archbishop took him by the hand and the two men warmly gazed at each other. The priest's eyes, dark pools of brown, shed tears of emotion. His wife stood by, simultaneously proud and fearful. Formerly team vicar, he was licensed that day for a ministry of continual prayer; what better ministry could there be?

The Rector was a humble, self-effacing man, a Donald Pleasance look-alike with many of the qualities of the Warden in the *Barchester Chronicles*. Clearly he had been the driving force in restoring some dilapidated buildings in the middle of the town, transforming them into a community centre and job-creation facilities. Surly market traders who had had to give up their pitch that day to enable parking for official cars mixed with sympathetic locals as the Archbishop declared the centre open.

Trainee caterers served a marvellous lunch, which the Archbishop combined with an interview with a reporter from the local radio station. Inevitably he was asked about the Thorpe Reprocessing Plant at Sellafield, enthusiastically approved by locals for providing much needed employment. He followed his maxim of 'When in Rome . . .' and enthused as well. Then came a walkabout through the town in the process of recovering its Georgian splendour, with bewildered truckers wondering who this purple-clad figure was who stopped the traffic.

The traffic wreaked its revenge; engine noise and sirens accompanied the electronic organ for an outdoor service celebrating three hundred years that had seen the church built, burned, and rebuilt. The Archbishop preached, inevitably taking us back to the 1960s. The Bishop of Carlisle was there too, and warmly welcomed us. One sweet comment of his made me smile: 'I haven't brought my chaplain,' he explained. 'I don't like to make him travel such long distances.' As we drove the long journey home I did wonder why Carlisle-to-Whitehaven chaplain transit is unacceptable whereas York-to-Whitehaven chaplain transit is OK. And he did not begin his day by chasing ducks.

We get some funny requests. A charming vicar on the Wolds, having invited the Archbishop to address a special service celebrating the family, asked for a further favour. A lavatory had recently been installed at the back of the church, and he wondered if the Archbishop would consecrate it on his visit. He added that the cost of installation had been met entirely by the fund-raising efforts of three old ladies.

The lot of devising prayers and orders of dedication generally falls to me, so often I have to be pretty inventive. I was tempted to devise a form on this occasion, along the lines of:

Introit:	Lord, *enthroned* in heavenly splendour . . .
Text:	To him that overcometh will I grant to sit with me on my *throne* (Revelation 3.21)
Prayer:	That we may be *flushed* with faith . . .
Recessional:	'Shine, Jesus, Shine' (to the tune of 'Three Old Ladies Locked in the Lavatory')

However, we played it safe and informed the good vicar that no consecration was necessary, since the loo was dedicated by transference by virtue of being affixed to an already consecrated building. This convincing piece of Canon Law actually originated with me and has since proved repeatedly invaluable.

The lavatory was quite an impressive construction, and even though we did not consecrate it, we much admired it. It would be useful for the predominantly young congregation should any toddlers feel a call other than one to discipleship.

The Archbishop's sermon had an admirable versatility about it. He began with quite a complex exposition on the doctrine of baptism, which was clearly not going down well. People's attention was drifting, children were crying. But he caught their attention by breaking off in mid-sentence, 'That baby's crying because it's bored; we too may be bored, but we're not allowed to cry.' He took this as his cue to elaborate on suppressed emotion, including religious yearnings that we may sublimate but which are nevertheless real, despite their apparent absence.

The congregation were gripped, so gripped that they missed a totally unintended *double entendre*. In discussing the present malaise with family life, the Archbishop made the priceless statement that the trouble with modern marriage was that 'Husbands and wives get on top of each other too much.' I bit a piece out of the inside of my cheek trying to suppress the emotion of helpless laughter. Whilst I am indebted that a lifelong connection with the church has taught me to yawn with my mouth closed, it has yet to furnish me with the ability to ward off fits of giggles.

Unintended humour aside, it was a good sermon not least because of John Habgood's ability to take soundings and act on them. Halfway through he gauged that the level was wrong and altered the pitch. In lectures on preaching the Archbishop stresses the need to be attentive to the type of congregation being addressed. It is good that he practises what he teaches when he preaches.

19 MAY

Potty training is no longer tolerated. In these politically correct days we have to use the proper name, Post Ordination Training (initials POT, hence the nickname), which is a pity. For the term Potty Training conferred a healthy lightness of touch on those years immediately after ordination when you were learning the ropes. It stopped you taking yourself and your future too seriously, all too aware that the ultimate purpose of potty training was to defecate to order.

The Archbishop hosts a day for Potty people annually, which gives him an opportunity to chat informally with his junior clergy as well as giving them food for thought. My first Potty Day was in the early eighties when both John Habgood and I were learning the ropes; he as an Archbishop, I as a clergyman. At coffee he sidled up to a small group of us; the conversation immediately died and a long silence ensued, punctuated at last by one line from the Archbishop, the gist of which being that my friend's new parish had more sheep than people. He then moved on to be silent with another group, but before he was out of earshot, my friend, a dour Teessider, passed comment: 'Chatty sort o' bloke, ain' he?' An example of hyperbole, I fear.

After lunch the Archbishop gathers his junior chicks into the drawing-room and, watched eagerly by his twentieth-century predecessors, gives a short talk. Year in year out he manages to be fresh and stimulating and to offer insight which will drive his hearers to reassess and deepen their ministry. That being granted, we do have our moments. One year the Archbishop began his spiel with the words: 'Let me tell you how things look from where I'm sitting.'

'Veeery niiice, Sah,' quipped a perky Scot, formerly very much an army man.

'How little you know,' responded the Archbishop, so icily that further witticism was quelled.

Another time the Archbishop felt pressurized into giving the junior troops a stiff talk about the subject of attraction in ministry, highlighting the sensitive situations where pastoral care spills over into emotional involvement. What he said about professionals living within boundaries of behaviour was actually very good and indicated a shrewd knowledge of how the world was and worked.

It was marred, however, by a time warp that cast him back to the 1950s, when all curates were pale young bachelors in their twenties, fodder for the wiles of women who wanted seduction and salvation in one package. I felt distinctly uneasy about what the middle-aged spinsters in our midst would make of his tips on how to avoid being compromised by a person of the female sex. And his solution—to visit women in the late morning or at lunch-time, but never, never at night—betrayed a quaint Cambridge gate-hours mentality. This assumed that sexual intercourse only took place between the hours of midnight and 6.0 a.m.; depriving male undergraduates of female company during those hours was therefore assumed to solve the problem.

All an age gone by. Sadly so. In a strange and yearning way I rejoiced that we had an Archbishop who was an ambassador for that past, reminding us of its proprieties. And surely proprieties is what potty training is all about . . .

29 MAY

Back in 1993 on this date we journeyed to Liverpool for the Battle of the Atlantic. Actually the battle had taken place fifty years before; today we would see no action other than marking its memories in Liverpool Cathedral. The Fleet, merchant shipping and the Royal Yacht *Brittania* had arrived at the port, but unfortunately had proved too big even for Liverpool Cathedral to accommodate them, so had to remain outside.

Even smaller vessels found difficulty breaking through the security net that had been thrown around Liverpool that day. I got there early and by shuffling passes of various hues was reluctantly allowed to drive through. Getting the enormous case containing the primatial cross past the security at the cathedral door proved more difficult; the officers obviously suspected they had before them a hybrid of Exocet® and bazooka, cushioned in blue velvet. Trying to explain to a policeman what a primatial cross is requires a fair bit of effort.

Once in the cathedral, I hung around near the entrance so I could vouch for the Archbishop. Even then, the security men were very puzzled by his mitre; I think we would have been better off pretending it was a tea cosy.

We fared better, though, than the Bishop of Liverpool. He was stopped at a roadblock and told that on no account could he proceed, despite protesting that he was the Diocesan, so really ought to be allowed to attend a service in his own cathedral. Eventually they let him through, but he arrived with only minutes to spare.

Before the service proper started, the dignitaries were presented to the Prince and Princess of Wales, whose presence explained the massive security. I stood behind the Archbishop and watched. The Prince was courteous, spoke in crisp sentences seasoned with humour and smile, his face ruddier and his height smaller than his media image. The Princess, on the other hand, matched hers, smartly turned out, with the persistent habit of addressing people by turning her head away and giving them a sidelong glance.

Memories of the service? The rousing fanfare, deafening for me sitting right next to the buglers. The standard-bearers of today's Armed Forces, marching proudly, taking their places, yet, when the moment came, *not* saying the Lord's Prayer virtually to a man. The old soldiers and old sailors, heart-wrenchingly frail, as they marched in time to present their mementoes at the altar. Their smartness and precision somehow made them seem all the more vulnerable. You wanted to rush up and embrace them with thanks.

The Archbishop alerted us in his sermon to the price that winning the Battle had exacted. On a 'Homes fit for Heroes' theme he mused on the present-day treatment of our shipyards and shipbuilders whose toil fifty years before had been an indispensable part of victory.

Then came the march past outside the cathedral by lines and lines of veterans, witnessed by the Prince and Princess. The Prince stood for well on half an hour, absolutely still, to attention, saluting each and every one, exuding deep gratitude. The Princess fell foul of a gale that had blown up. With one hand she held onto her hat, in a quasi-salute; with the other she held down her flimsy skirt. With no other hands free, she had to pass her handbag to the Dean, who clutched it rather self-consciously, all too aware of scornful glances from the muscular men around him.

It was a tremendous day in many ways. One felt for those who had died and those who had survived. One felt for the Prince and Princess, with all the media attention, all the disappointments: two people who exuded loveliness but at the same time seemed as deeply wounded as those frail veterans.

4 JUNE

It was brave of the vicar to mark Pentecost with such verve. Each of those whom the Archbishop confirmed released helium-filled balloons high into the air, symbolizing the soaring of the Spirit. In addition, two white doves were freed from their cages and rose with wings violently fluttering, evoking the coming of the Spirit in the form of a dove at our Lord's baptism.

I need to add that all this frantic activity happened outside after the service and not during it. Even then, I was not sure about the doves. Doves and pigeons seem to have been alighting on the Church (which is the body of Christ, after all) ever since our Lord's baptism. As someone who has had to clear belfries of kilos of guano, I definitely feel that when the dove landed on Jesus in the Jordan, it set an unfortunate precedent.

But no guano fell on us today, and the vicar's verve paid off. A truly happy end to a confirmation. Perhaps the *Son of ASB* could include a rubric at the service end: 'Now balloons and doves may be released; protective headgear may be worn.' So that is why bishops wear mitres!

Our Whitsunday still had good things in store, a trip to *Heartbeat* country for a Festival of Science and the Sacred, a subject to warm the Archbishop's heart. As we set off I realized he was pronouncing our destination, Grosmont, as Grocemont (which should be pronounced Growmont). I had to say in a loud voice to Gordon, 'Which route are we taking to Grosmont?' and 'Isn't it a steam festival this week in Grosmont?'

Eventually the Archbishop got the message and said, 'Ah yes, Grosmont, as in the French.' Embarrassment was averted, though not without cost. The Archbishop obviously felt that having conceded one point of omniscience he could give away no more. He therefore refused to believe you could see Roseberry Topping from the Whitby side of the North York Moors, when I *knew* you could. 'It must be another hill,' he said, getting out an OS map which he just happened to have stuffed in his cassock pocket. No other hill in all creation could look like Roseberry Topping, but I said nothing; honour was clearly at stake.

Grosmont was a poppet of a place. The local choir consisted of a jolly bunch of ladies, decked in thick woollen robes designed to keep out the winter chill which pervaded the vale. Not so useful on this balmy spring evening.

The service was a veritable feast. As well as the local choir, none less than Leeds Parish Church Choir squeezed into the choir stalls and performed full Sung Evensong with sundry poets springing up and reciting their works. All very entertaining, except I prefer my verse to be blank. I always feel that hymn writers are exceedingly restricted by having to make their theology rhyme; after all, there are only so many words which rhyme with God.

The service over, we lingered to look at the display of artwork and sculpture. Amazing to think that this tiny village could put on such a festival. Though I have to admit that I do not go for art in a big way, so I stole away and watched the steam trains huffing and puffing by the church side. Now they really had the breath of God about them!

LAST DAYS

A candlelit dinner in the Great Hall casts an inevitable atmosphere. The occasion is a farewell to one of the Senior Staff. The Archbishop makes a gracious speech, the retiring cleric makes a gracious reply: the tensions of diocesan life at the top dissolve as we mourn the loss of a true friend.

On these occasions my mind is prone to wander away from polite conversation. The portraits of archbishops from across the centuries seem to come alive in the ghostly candlelight and distract me. What do they think of all this?

There's Accepted Frewen (imagine your mum calling you in to tea with a Christian name like that) who seems to disdain it all. He disdained his Puritan parents who gave him such an odd Christian name; yet he carried their Puritan baggage in that he had a lifelong aversion to women, allowing none in the Palace whatsoever. He therefore looks very disapprovingly indeed at all these chattering clergy wives, whilst casting a rare look of admiration at George Austin. But disdain is his hallmark; he even manages a sneer at the ancient electric radiator, sizzling in the grate below him.

'Who are you sneering at, you old prude?!' shouts Lancelot Blackburn, banished to a corner of the room. Before becoming Archbishop he was none less than chaplain to a pirate ship. Clearly the Crown Appointments' Commission made a slip with this one. One thing has always puzzled me: what did a chaplain to a pirate ship do?

I can just imagine him announcing the notices in typically Anglican fashion: 'Next Sunday as follows, me hearties: 8.0 a.m. Recovery from hangover; 10.0 a.m. Holy Communion; 11.30 a.m. Rape and pillage; 2.0 p.m. Walking the plank; 6.0 p.m. Evensin.' Or maybe he forgot his priestly origins and threw in his lot with the baddies. His swarthy looks make that seem the most likely. He casts his eye up and down the table, disappointed that he can only find two fetching maidens under the age of fifty. Intriguingly, the present Archbishop cites Blackburn as his favourite predecessor: perhaps there is more to John Habgood than meets the eye.

Vernon Harcourt's eyes are at half-mast. Archbishop for forty years with sixteen children, he is ready for bed, wearied of ecclesiastical intrigue and domestic turmoil. He saw it all; nothing can surprise him.

Unlike Richard Scrope, who was surprised to have his head chopped off. He had been a great buddy of Richard II, close enough to him to encourage him to abdicate when the going got rough. He soon lived to regret his advice as Richard's successor, Henry IV (definitely Part I and Part II) gave the North East short shrift. As archbishops are wont to do, Scrope commandeered a force of men- (mostly priests-at-arms) to protest. They vastly outnumbered the King's men, whom they faced west of York. Which was when they made their big mistake. In return for laying down their arms they were promised that their grievances would be heard and be resolved.

It is frankly amazing how many times in English history that trick has been played; yet still people are taken in, lock, stock, and barrel. The disarmed Scrope was immediately arrested, tried, and beheaded in York's Knavesmire. Since his trial was in this very Great Hall, you can understand his distress: 'In this place where I was unfairly condemned to die thou darest to consume fowl and boiled potatoes?' (Since potatoes had yet to be introduced to fourteenth-century Europe, one has to allow a little artistic licence at this point; Shakespeare would have approved.)

Edwin Sandys was clearly at ease with the very same domesticity which so offended Scrope, since he is the first (and only) archbishop to be portrayed with his poker-faced wife. Ostensibly this was because he was the first married archbishop, in Elizabeth I's reign. But there is a sub-agenda of scandal. Sandys refused to cede much-coveted land (in the surprising vicinity of Doncaster) to an avaricious fellow called Stapleton. The latter, taking his cue from the story of Potiphar's wife in Genesis 39, developed a cunning plan. Whilst Sandys was staying with him, he induced his own wife to visit the sleeping archbishop in his bedchamber. Stapleton then 'discovered' them both and threatened to publicize the scandal unless the lands were handed over. But Sandys refused to give way to blackmail and was exonerated by Royal Council. They only had to look at his portrait for mitigation. He was clearly incapable of doing anything improper (or proper for that matter) with his own wife, let alone anyone else's.

Rachel, my own wife, brought me back to the present century with a characteristically sharp observation, 'If you didn't know already, would you ever guess that this lot were bishops and senior clergy?' She certainly had a point, since the Senior Staff, having a much needed break from being holy, certainly were not flaunting their godliness as they swigged the wine. All that is, except one, whose portrait one day would hang with his predecessors and talk to chaplains in time to come.

19 JUNE

To a holiday camp on the bracing east coast of Lincolnshire for a Diocesan Clergy Conference. The place had been much recommended by the Secretary for Mission and Ministry. He had stayed there for a weekend to suss it out as a possible diocesan venue and had thoroughly enjoyed it, 'Even the cabaret with Freddie Starr,' he enthusiastically informed the Archbishop.

'Freddie who?' the Archbishop inevitably replied, deadpan.

We went the scenic route via Scunthorpe and Grimsby, the Archbishop driving. As we neared our destination, our hearts fell at the sight of miles on miles of barbed wire encircling our home for the next few days.

Along with three hundred other clergy, we parked, checked in, and traversed the camp, looking for our billet. The Senior Staff were housed in luxury accommodation—they had only agreed to the conference being there on that condition. Actually their accommodation was akin to a part of my former parish in Middlesbrough affectionately known as the H-Blocks. The lesser clergy were housed in tenements, now that these were no longer needed for the set of *Tenko*. These properties were far superior to those enjoyed by camp staff, which had the look of dog kennels about them.

The week certainly saw life in all its fullness. Thousands of holiday-makers who were not ordained were determined to enjoy themselves and danced and drank and sang and played until the early hours. Some clergy joined them; some shunned them. A couple of clergy's chalets were broken into: one lost a tape recorder, another a hair-dryer. 'A hair-dryer?!' exploded the Archbishop in his best Lady Bracknell voice when he heard about it. 'A hair-dryer! What on earth is a clergyman doing with a hair-dryer?' I guess he was thinking of those massive things they have at hairdressers and had never been acquainted with the hand-held variety.

The Archbishop's lectures were by far a highlight of the whole proceedings, primarily because he came across as a Diocesan who knew his clergy and was known by them. He seemed remarkably relaxed and at ease through it all, oblivious to all the tackiness. I suppose it took him back to his public school days.

He did not even flinch at the daily Eucharist, celebrated in the Gaiety Theatre of all places, with the celebrant on stage, flanked by two giant stallions carrying knights in shining armour. We only had to substitute 'the Lord be with you' with 'Hi-di-hi' and our joy would have been complete. When it came to the administration of communion the cast (sorry, assistants) descended from the stage to the audience (sorry, congregation) like a music-hall turn determined to go for the ultimate in audience participation. One woman assistant dressed in cassock and surplice had trouble negotiating the steps from the stage, primarily because she had a chalice in one hand and a large handbag in the other (enter Lady Bracknell again).

The weather was perfect, and even tempted you to tunnel under the barbed wire in search of the sea. Just as well the weather was good with all the traipsing about from venue to venue we had to do. The final Eucharist was accompanied by a torrential downpour. As George Austin remarked, 'It was the Lord reminding us just how awful the week would have been had the weather been against us.'

24 JUNE

To Sheffield again. We outfoxed the super-tram upheavals and arrived at the cathedral in good time for a service to commission new Church Army officers. I suppose the best definition of such an officer is an unordained minister who specializes in evangelism. Today's service was redeemed from being a downbeat ordination by its sheer unstuffiness matched by the enthusiasm and vitality of the young people being commissioned. They sang their hearts out and meant it.

Memories of the morning include a severely deaf candidate whose alertness and integrity was so vivid as to be contagious. The final hymn, 'And can it be that I should gain an interest in the Saviour's blood?' was sung as we processed out with the candidates into the vestries. Normally as such a procession leaves the main body of the church, it stops singing. These candidates continued in time and in tune; I hope their singing never stops.

The Archbishop caught all this in his talk; since it was John the Baptist's birthday he took the Baptist as his theme, drawing parallels with John's role and the role of these new officers. His clear sentences and illustrations betrayed a tremendous empathy for the Church Army's work and the joys and stresses that lay ahead for these new candidates.

The opening sentence for the Eucharist for this day made me catch my breath. The Archbishop said in his usual measured tones: 'There was a man sent by God whose name was John.' Indeed there was; and is.

Inevitably even a man sent from God did not please everyone. Having cast off my robes and donned my suit, I went to an excellent lunch at the Church Army College. I sat next to a newly commissioned officer and his parents. 'Where do you come from then?' was my chat up line, displaying great originality.

'We come from Somerset,' the mother replied, answering for

her son. 'We were so disappointed that it was the Archbishop of York and not Canterbury doing our Paul. You see, we knew him when he was at Bath and Wells; he'd have done it so much better.'

I ate in silence. 'Where do you come from?' asked the mother, returning my question.

I looked straight at her and said with as much ice as I could summon, 'York.' Then their eyes were opened, and they recognized me, and the enormity of their gaffe dawned. I disappeared from their sight and left their hearts (and consciences) to burn.

25 JUNE

To Oswestry, where good King Oswald of Northumbria fought his last battle, his body dismembered and nailed to sundry stakes (hence Oswestry = Oswald's tree?). Apparently as he fell, mortally wounded, unpreoccupied with his own fate, the saint prayed for the souls of his soldiers.

Given the adverse reception the Welsh borders had extended to Oswald, not surprisingly we approached the area with a little trepidation. The journey was long and we had to water our steed at Wrexham, using the break to pop into a Little Chef.

Such restaurants are packed on Sunday afternoons and today was no exception. Cassocked Archbishop and chaplain together with uniformed chauffeur were shown to a tiny table by a bemused waitress. There was soon more space because within minutes the whole café cleared, with other punters clearly deciding they would get out while the going was good. You never know what might happen when an Archbishop and his chaplain ride into town.

The Archbishop encouraged us to order whatever we wanted, no expense spared. We had been on the road for a while and were all hungry, so I was just about to suggest the Maxi-breakfast when Gordon chipped in and opened the bidding, 'I'll just have a toasted teacake and a cup of tea, thank you, your Grace.' (The latter form of address ensured that any remaining customers made a sharp exit.)

Having been shamed by Gordon's modesty, we all ended up having teacake and tea. Mind you, he had a bumper picnic secreted in the boot to consume whilst we were in church. Such a luxury was denied the Archbishop and me, who would have to make do solely with that Little Chef snack between our leaving home at 1.0 p.m. and returning twelve hours later.

Whilst Gordon filled the tank, the Archbishop was so intrigued by a nearby car wash that he peered through its window, acutely interested at the progress of a car going through the various stages. What the driver of the car thought as he saw an archiepiscopal form loom amidst the water jets, I cannot imagine.

Oswestry church was a splendid place, the service well ordered and produced. Afterwards the *crème de la crème* of the congregation were to have a special dinner at a nearby hotel to celebrate. 'What a terrible shame you can't join us,' the vicar remarked. 'But we know you want to get off with such a long drive ahead of you.' Never mind about the long journey; I would have given my right arm for just a sniff at one of the lush courses. I guess the Archbishop would have as well.

Having made our farewells, the well-replenished Gordon took us towards the setting sun on a tour of Offa's Dyke. Eventually we realized that the setting sun was not the ideal direction for our eastward journey home, so we did a further detour through the winding roads of the Welsh borders. At least we had escaped with our lives. Poor Oswald! I bet he'd had a decent meal, though, before being hacked to death.

1 JULY

Another Open Day, with the Archbishop and his staff selling and guiding in aid of charity. I act as a guide myself and thoroughly enjoy these occasions for the wide cross-section of people we encounter. I show them with pride my favourite room, the drawing-room, perfectly proportioned Strawberry Hill Gothic. The style was copied from Walpole's house at Strawberry Hill, Twickenham, when Mrs Archbishop admired the place and presumably pestered her husband until she got one. Which is why we have a palace with an eighteenth-century front and a thirteenth-century back. I suppose it set the craze for extensions.

In the drawing-room one feels terribly watched, since it contains the very vivid portraits of all the twentieth-century archbishops. Maclagan saw the century in and is famed for introducing to the Diocese those twin evils, Sunday schools and the Mother's Union. Next comes Cosmo Gordon Lang, who was found practising his signature, Cosmo Cantuar, whilst still at theological college. He did not like his portrait (which hangs over the fireplace—Sicilian marble), describing it to Hensley Henson, Bishop of Durham, as making him look pompous, prelatical, and proud. Ever controversial, the Bishop of Durham replied, 'And which of these three epithets does your Grace take exception to?'

Lang went on to Canterbury; Henson remained at Durham.

Next comes William Temple, a cuddly teddy bear of a man with a wide vision of social justice. Although a much respected philosopher and biblical scholar, he managed to retain his humanity.

As did Cyril Garbett, who became archbishop at the tender age of seventy. Age did not diminish his vigour—in the middle of the last war, he flew to Moscow to express solidarity with our Russian allies. In his eighties he went on a three-month tour of the Antipodes, describing how he was carried ashore in Papua New Guinea by six burly natives, the surf whipping their muscular limbs. On the beach two thousand natives knelt for his blessing. Some tour; which makes his advice in a diocesan newsletter ring a little hollow: 'When you go on holiday, don't go too far and don't do too much. Otherwise you'll return more exhausted than when you began.'

Garbett died at eighty-four to be succeeded by the 52-year-old Michael Ramsey, who *always* looked eighty-four. If we have the same age gap with the present archbishop, his successor will be thirty-six, which puts me out of the running. Ramsey's eyebrows danced with the delight of God. A fidget to say the least, his portrait artist gave up on him, painted his head and then got the village bobby to model the rest. Which explains the policeman's boot sticking out of the cope, the ultimate in undercover work. Ramsey stands as my all-time favourite archbishop.

Donald Coggan's portrait makes him look a cold figure, which is opposite from the truth, since he was a warm man who knew his clergy and people intimately. I was seriously injured in a road accident when I was fifteen; the morning after the accident, there was a letter on my bedside table from Donald Coggan, including a feeble joke and his best wishes. People do not forget care like that.

Stuart Blanch's portrait is different from the rest. It depicts him perched on his study chair, Bible and dictaphone in hand, with red telephone by his side (a hotline to God or Lambeth?). The study wall falls away to reveal the river, power station, and cooling towers beyond. In the midst of all this frantic activity sits a very relaxed man; for me Stuart Blanch's achievement was that he inspired me to ease off and not see myself as indispensable. Apparently he had a filing cabinet marked 'too difficult' into which he put a fair few problems that come an archbishop's way. Psychologically it was a good ploy, since by filing them he felt he had actually *done* something! And he was continually surprised how many problems never re-emerged.

John Habgood sits in the corner, twinkly-eyed, bemused,

able to spy on all the rest from his vantage point. He was painted by the same artist who painted Ramsey, which seems fitting since in many ways he has inherited Ramsey's mantle. At the opposite end of the room one panel remains empty, reserved for the portrait of his successor. When the room was built in the 1760s, how did they know that there would be exactly the right number of panels for the twentieth-century archbishops? One is almost driven to revisit God's providence.

A room full of holy men. Since we are surrounded by so great a cloud of witnesses let us run with perseverance the race that is set before us.

2 JULY

To end is to begin. In St Peter's Minster, near St Peter's Day, the Archbishop of York will ordain about a dozen deacons. Significantly, one of his last acts before his retirement will be to breathe new life into the Church by commissioning these new ministers. Their surplices will be fresh, crisply ironed, and dazzling white, as dazzling as their expectations, as yet unsullied by the frustrations, heartbreak, and sheer slog of ministry.

They will be ordained by one who—though made deacon over forty years before—has kept his vision fresh, his faith fed and enlarged by prayer, his mind attuned to the mind of Christ by relentless study, recasting the tenets of Christian doctrine afresh for his own generation. Each word he utters of the Ordination and Eucharist which follows will sound as if it had been long pondered and found to have immense weight, a gravity conveyed by his intonation. There will be no false *bonhomie*; he will shake hands with few people at the Peace. Yet it will seem he enfolds the whole congregation in invisible embrace.

There will be no slick grins, but rather a timid smile which will invade the whole of his face. He will generate a sense of awe, almost fearfulness for what lies ahead for those he commissions this day. Yet the gentle smile proclaims the victory which will be theirs if only they hold to the God he has held to and still holds to. Each ordinand that day could make no better prayer than to receive a portion of the Spirit which has invaded John Habgood's whole being.